I Would Be Loved

LINDA J. FALKNER

"I Would be Loved" by Linda Falkner. ISBN 1-58939-164-0 (softcover).

Published 2002 by Virtualbookworm.com Publishing Inc., P.O. Box 9949, College Station, TX , 77842, US. © 2002 Linda Falkner. All rights reserved. No part of this publication may be reproduced, stored in a retrieval system, or transmitted in any form or by any means, electronic, mechanical, recording or otherwise, without the prior written permission of Linda Falkner.

Manufactured in the United States of America.

TABLE OF CONTENTS

NOBODY'S CHILDREN – PART 2

PART 1

PROLOGUE

The three children watch a television movie about a child, living on a magic island, who never grows up. Alice, my first born, and Ben, my youngest, sit motionless with fascination. The third child, Pixie, wiggles nonstop, repositioning herself every few seconds.

She came to me only a month earlier, just before her nineteenth birthday. A foster child who had "aged out" out the system, Pixie was also a "drug baby" with Fetal Alcohol Syndrome, who was born before anyone knew there was such a thing. She was emotionally, physically, and sexually abused, both in and out of foster care.

Pixie has multiple and overlapping problems. Her life is one answer to the question, "What happens to these kids when they grow up?" She is seriously damaged, but she is not alone. Her story is typical of many prenatally drug and alcohol exposed children.

I attempt to give Pixie guidance and support as she struggles, fighting to pass from the innocence of childhood into the adult world. But it becomes clearer to me each day that this is a battle she cannot win. The damage from the alcohol and a lifetime of abuse and foster care is too great for her to overcome.

Oh honey, I think, *I wish there was a magical place where you could be happy in your perpetual childhood.*

Pixie abandons her attempt to watch the movie and paces back and forth between the kitchen and family room, yelling her displeasure at some imagined slight. Since moving in, Pixie has balanced fun with disruption, happiness with anger. She can't sit still and is often frustrating and demanding. Although I wonder how much longer I can keep her in my family, I strive to hold on because she desperately needs a family's care. But more than that, something special about this child/adult has touched my heart with love.

Babies are magical beings,
who come from fairy laughter.

IN THE BEGINNING

I n the beginning there were pictures of abused children and stories in the newspaper. There were advertisements painted on bus stop benches asking people to become foster parents, and a woman in the park bringing her foster children to play. In the beginning the thought of caring for a foster child was merely a spark in my imagination.

This was the time when crack cocaine was new and addicted infants were abandoned in hospitals for months and sometimes years. The mothers were too involved in this new drug to care for their children, and foster homes couldn't open fast enough.

My husband, Gary, and I discussed being foster parents at length. Although we were apprehensive about caring for a difficult or impaired child, we decided to apply for a foster care license. Since I was already an at-home mother to Alice, aged six, and Ben, aged three, one more would fit right into our life, or so we thought...

Children's Protective Services (CPS) scheduled their

training class for licensing foster parents in a university building, one of many look-alike structures along a twisting street. *I wonder if CPS deliberately makes it difficult to find the classroom to discourage all but the most committed-or foolish?* I thought as Gary and I drove along several winding streets.

After circling for half an hour, we finally arrived for the CPS training. The spacious meeting room had long tables arranged in a U-shape facing a large chalkboard. A coffee pot brewing on a corner table sent forth a welcome smell. The table arrangement gave us a clear view of the other people. We were a mixed group-old, young, Black, White, Hispanic-dressed in suits and old jeans, married and single.

Although we came from different backgrounds, each of us had one important thing in common-we loved children and wanted to do something meaningful to help them. Gary and I sat next to a middle-aged couple who smiled and seemed pleasant.

"Find yourselves a seat," the instructor said.

I instantly liked this friendly, easygoing woman who emanated warmth and trust. The newspaper reports about CPS made the workers sound like mechanized bureaucrats, incompetent, and uncaring. However, here was a competent, excellent teacher, not at all what reporters portrayed. I later learned the newspapers weren't all wrong; she was merely one the system hadn't been burned out-yet.

The instructor introduced herself as Abigail, our licensing worker. "I won't be teaching you parenting skills, which I assume you already know," she explained. "This class is to teach you about foster children and Children's Protective Services. Our children come into shelter care because they are endangered in their own homes. We often pick them up in the middle of the night. The law requires a court hearing within twenty-four hours to determine if they should go back home, stay with a relative, or be placed in shelter care." Abigail continued, "Children may stay in a shelter home for up to six weeks. Then, if the problems with their parents haven't been resolved, they are given a more permanent status-foster care-which can last as long as eighteen months.

"The birth parents sign a contract agreeing to do

certain things, such as taking a parent training class, keeping a safe, clean home, and having a source of income." Abigail listed each requirement on the chalkboard as she talked. I took careful notes.

"The mothers of cocaine exposed infants must complete a drug treatment program," she continued. "CPS promises to return their children when the contract is completed. The law limits a child's' stay in foster care to eighteen months. After that, the child must be placed in a permanent home, either going back to the mother, living with relatives, or adoption.

"This is what the law says and it's an ideal we try to meet, but it doesn't always work out as neatly in real life. In addition, what you are learning only applies to this county. Each state and each county in this state have a different system. There are great variations between them."

The hours passed quickly. During the coffee break, I talked to the couple sitting next to me. Ruth and Joseph were returning to foster care after having quit some time earlier. They had experience working with emotionally disturbed teenagers and wanted to care for adolescents again.

"We were burned out and needed the break," Ruth explained.

"Emotionally disturbed adolescents sound difficult," I said. "I'm not surprised you burned out. I'd feel really uncomfortable with them."

"It wasn't the kids. We left due to problems with the bureaucracy," Joseph added.

Engrossed in conversation, the break ended all too quickly. Ruth and I exchanged phone numbers so we could chat later.

During the second part of class Abigail taught us more about the children.

"Our children have been suddenly uprooted and removed from their parents, and then moved from home to home within the system." Abigail called the foster children "our children," as though they belonged to CPS.

"At first they have a honeymoon period where they behave like angels, but it doesn't take long until pre-existing problems such as lying, stealing, tantrums, fighting, or smearing feces reappear. With each move, they have a shorter honeymoon period and their troubled behavior, or acting out, becomes worse. It's not unusual to move some kids three or four times a year because foster parents can't handle them."

This made me glad I'd requested an infant. At that time, I never expected, or wanted, children old enough to act this way.

The next week Abigail talked about abuse reports. "Almost every parent in foster care can expect to be investigated for abuse. Ninety percent of these reports are unfounded-or in bureaucratic terms, dropped for lack of evidence."

While Abigail was never guilty of this, I later met CPS workers who used the term "unfounded" to imply the foster parent's guilt even when there was no evidence of abuse. CPS *never* used the word, "innocent."

Abigail continued, "Teenagers in foster care often call the abuse line hoping an investigation will allow them to return to their parents, which almost all children prefer to foster care. Children know that even the worst parents love them and parents are devastated when their kids are taken away by force. It's not surprising many angry parents call the abuse line when they notice a slight bump or bruise on their child during visitation, especially if the child was removed because of bruises. These investigations are part of being a foster parent. If you feel you can't handle them, then you shouldn't be in foster care. Go home and think it over carefully."

I did think about it, but I guess Gary and I didn't really believe it would ever happen to us. The other people in the class must have been more realistic because the next week several couples were absent.

One week the subject was cocaine exposed infants. "Many of these infants are abandoned in the hospital at birth," Abigail said. "These babies are very irritable and may cry for hours. They can't tolerate much stimulation and dislike being held or played with. They need a quiet room with plain white walls. Even when they no longer need specialized nursing care the hospital is stuck boarding them at taxpayers' expense.

These 'boarder babies' are becoming a more serious and expensive problem every year."

Gary and I had originally planned on taking a cocaine exposed infant but the idea of taking a child with Fetal Alcohol Syndrome, a major cause of birth defects and mental retardation, never occurred to us, and was never mentioned. As we learned more, we began having second thoughts about taking a drug-exposed child. At times our house shook with the children's uproar. Alice jumped and sang while Ben loved making loud train imitations. No, we'd be better off with a normal child.

Finally, classes ended. Less than half the people who started the class graduated eight weeks later. Now, through individual interviews, the number of participants would again be reduced. Abigail gave Gary and me a thick questionnaire asking about our family history and life style, which we then discussed with her. She asked Alice and Ben to draw pictures of themselves with a foster child. Alice drew a picture of everyone holding hands. Three-year-old Ben drew a train scribble. Babies didn't interest him.

Children's Protective Services checked our references, including Alice's elementary school grades and behavior reports. We were fingerprinted at the police department. We had our house tested for radon gas. CPS inspected our fire extinguishers and required me to draw and post emergency escape plans. Our family even had to have a fire drill. It seemed CPS did everything short of dissecting us.

Then we waited. Nearly a year had passed since I first called Children's Protective Services. Where were all those children desperately needing homes? Had we been forgotten? Finally I called Abigail.

"You don't have a baby yet?" she asked, surprised. "I'll see what I can find out."

Four hours later, the phone rang...

*Drug-exposed babies are incredibly expensive to care for.
These children overwhelm hospitals, child protective services,
foster care, schools and every other support system involved
with their care.*

SOMETHING'S WRONG
WITH THIS BABY

"Hello, Mrs. Falkner, I'm calling from Children's Protective Services. We have a little ten-month-old girl for you named Valentine. She's been in the hospital recovering from an injury and is being released today. Can you take her?"

Although I'd been expecting a newborn, I only hesitated a second -- excitement froze the words in my throat.

"Yes," I whispered.

I loved Valentine from the first moment I saw her. When she came to me without hesitation, I felt euphoric but surprised. *How different from my own babies,* I thought. *They clung to me and cried when strangers approached. Now I'm the stranger but she's not the least bit afraid."*

The caseworker handed me a thin folder containing information on the baby and left.

She's so cute, I thought as I held the chubby baby at arms length to observe her. She had an angelic face framed with brown curly hair, a small upturned nose, and wide set eyes. I didn't realize until after the caseworker left that she had no teeth and her upper lip was flattened and thin, like Grandma's when she removes her dentures. When I held Valentine close, she felt soft and floppy like a rag doll, but she didn't want to be held and wiggled to get down on the floor.

Dianne, a long time friend who worked as a psychiatric nurse, came to see her. "What an odd looking child," she said.

"She's beautiful," I answered defensively. Valentine appeared normal if you didn't look too closely, and I wasn't ready to admit anything was wrong with this baby, yet.

Alice was excited about having a sister. She wanted to be the first to give her a bottle, but to Alice's dismay, Valentine pulled away from her and struggled to get down. The baby wouldn't make eye contact. She turned her head or rolled her eyes to avoid looking at Alice. Both Gary and I tried giving her a bottle with the same results. Valentine grasped the bottle and made it clear she didn't want anyone to hold her.

She must have been terribly neglected, I thought. *She doesn't even know how to cuddle. Well, in this house she'll get lots of love and cuddling. She'll learn.*

I remember my children standing in their cribs calling "mama," as they raised their arms to be picked up, so I had a funny *something's wrong* feeling the next morning when I found Valentine sitting quietly in the crib showing no interest in anything.

"Hi, Baby! Do you want to come out?" I waited for her to raise her arms. She looked past me, apparently not understanding. To my disappointment, she didn't reach for me that day, or for many days to come.

———

It was ironic, I'd waited so long for this baby and only three days later received a call from a different caseworker asking me to take another child. But as she began describing the child and the injury that put the baby in foster care, I realized she was talking about Valentine.

"Is the child's name Valentine?" I asked.

"Yes, how did you know?"

"I got her three days ago when the doctor released her

from the hospital."

"Are you sure? She's not supposed to be released until today. It says so in this paper."

This was my first of many troubling experiences where Children's Protective Services had trouble communicating, even within itself.

When she arrived, Valentine had the symptoms of a bad cold. As time went on she continued having a stuffy, runny nose. Every morning, matter gummed her eyes shut and I had to pat them open with a warm washcloth.

"Yucky!" Ben commented as he watched me wash crusted goop from her face.

Valentine's folder was incomplete and contained meager information. There was no Medicaid card, something all the doctors required before seeing a child. The caseworker responsible for getting the card was unavailable. I called repeatedly until I finally reached her a week later.

"I've just started this job and have been in training," she said. "Valentine's the first child I've ever placed."

I didn't receive the Medicaid card until ten days after the baby arrived, an experience which taught me never to accept a child without first checking the folder. When a placement is dependent upon it, the caseworker can always find time to fill out the necessary paperwork.

This only partially solved the problem because the Medicaid card expired every month. Then, it usually took between ten and fifteen days to get a new one, if I got one at all. After about six months I began receiving the card regularly, often for children no longer in my care. (Happily, this situation has since changed and now Medicaid gives permanent plastic cards, which stay with the children. The recent use of HMO's or Medicaid managed care has also improved the availability of services.)

One morning, Valentine woke up with a thick yellow discharge draining from her ears. I couldn't put off taking her to a doctor any longer, but neither the caseworker nor her supervisor knew which doctors or clinics accepted Medicaid. Using the phone book, I called doctors and clinics until I found a clinic that took her insurance. It was located halfway across town and closed at noon.

"Bring her in right away," the doctor said. He had a heavy foreign accent and I had to concentrate to understand him. After briefly examining Valentine, he wrote a prescription for antibiotics.

"Bring her back in a week if she's not better."

I brought her back the next week, and the next, and the week after that. A month later she still wasn't better.

Not only was Valentine constantly sick, but she also didn't seem to be growing normally either mentally or physically. This became very obvious to me one morning when I took her grocery shopping She sat balanced precariously in the cart holding on with both hands while I held onto her with one hand to prevent her from falling. Ahead of me in the checkout line, a baby slightly larger than Valentine sat easily, babbled, and carried on a nonsensical conversation with her mother. Valentine rarely babbled.

"How old is she?" I asked.

"Seven months," the mother said.

Four months younger than Valentine.

"Is she big for her age?"

"She's about average," the mother replied.

I know children develop at different ages, but Valentine was much slower than most. I was concerned.

At eleven months Valentine finally began sitting alone, but she still didn't babble, make eye contact, or tolerate cuddling from adults. She enjoyed other children and loved watching Ben and Alice play. They loved entertaining her with singing and silly antics.

Although she interacted with my children, Valentine still kept her distance from me and other adults. Not only was her behavior odd, but her features were unusual enough that strangers asked me what was wrong. I didn't know how to answer them. Her flat face and wide set eyes were distinctive.

Her doctor didn't seem concerned. When I asked him to do a developmental evaluation, he patted me on the shoulder and said she'd outgrow it. I remember when I worked as a speech therapist years earlier, I'd met handicapped children who hadn't received therapy until their treatable problems became permanent. When I asked their mothers about the delay in their treatment, they would explain, "My doctor told me to wait for him to outgrow it, but he only got worse."

I felt patronized and put-off so I decided to get a second opinion. When the next doctor also reassured me everything was fine, and I should stop worrying, I called the caseworker.

"The doctors say everything's fine but I'm still concerned. She seems slow. What services are available to help her?"

Fortunately, the caseworker was also concerned and arranged an evaluation by a child development specialist. During the testing, Valentine would not imitate any activity, lost interest quickly, and still avoided eye contact. She didn't respond to her name, or any other words, and made few sounds.

"She's several months delayed and eye avoidance isn't normal at any age." The examiner showed me Valentine's test results. "I'm going to recommend more testing. You'll need to enroll her at CPS's (Children's Protective Services) medical clinic. I'm not sure what, but something's wrong with this baby."

Specialists from several different areas of expertise called a multidisciplinary, or M-team, evaluated her a few weeks later. The tests found a mild hearing loss due to ear infections, and a delay in physical and mental development, and growth. The M-team gave me several recommendations and a list of special schools.

I visited each program on the list before I chose Little Bits Day School. "High risk" children could begin attending at one year of age and Valentine's first birthday was only a week away. The M-team also assigned an infant stimulation teacher to come to my house once a week. Her job was to teach Gary and me how to help Valentine.

We had a birthday party for Valentine over the weekend. Gary helped Alice and Ben make decorations. My friend, Dianne, came with her two children. The baby sat in her high chair, smiled, and eyed the large chocolate cake. When I put a slice on her plate she cautiously stuck her finger in to taste it and flashed a wide toothless grin. Soon she succeeded in smearing chocolate cake and frosting all over her face and hair. Then the older children began imitating her, smearing chocolate frosting on each other's faces and laughing. Soon all five giggly imps were covered with chocolate frosting. After we got them cleaned up, I had small gifts for the kids. Ben rolled his present, a tiny toy car, along the floor while Valentine watched. Later she rolled the car herself, copying him. This is an important milestone because babies learn from imitation.

Valentine started school the next week at Little Bits Day School. Situated in a shopping mall, the classrooms were small but painted in bright cheery colors. The teacher had a degree in special education and worked with each child individually while aides played learning games with the other children. There were only six children in her class so Valentine received close attention.

"She's delightful!" the van driver exclaimed as Valentine flopped in her arms and offered a big toothless smile. The driver picked Valentine up each morning and when she brought her home in the afternoon, she passed along pleasant comments from the teacher. I liked this school and their staff and felt confident they could give my baby the help she needed to catch up with other children her age.

Once a week an infant stimulation teacher, Karen, came to my house to work with us.

"Sit her on the floor and run your fingers up her back. See how it helps her sit straight? She needs to learn to balance better. She has trouble because of her hypotonic, or floppy, muscle tone," she said.

Karen brought a giant bright orange rubber ball, sat the baby on it, held her, and rolled the ball gently so Valentine was forced to balance herself to keep upright. Valentine smiled and laughed as she learned how to straighten her back and use her muscles correctly.

Next, Karen rolled a beach ball to her. "Ball, here's a ball, Valentine. Ball. Roll the ball. Ball. Give me the ball."

After ten minutes, Karen changed the game
Valentine the ball and a shoe.

"Give me the *ball*, Valentine," she said.

Valentine stared blankly at her. The ball started to roll.

"Get the ball Valentine," Karen pointed.

Valentine still looked blank. Then she picked up the shoe and smiled. Karen seemed concerned.

"I don't really know what's wrong with her," she said later. "She's fourteen months old and should understand gestures like pointing to the ball. I think her physical development is all right now, but she doesn't understand any words -- not even her name -- and the sounds she makes are like a six month old. The problem isn't her hearing because even deaf children understand gestures.

I worked with Valentine daily using the ball and the methods Karen taught me. She made slow but regular progress sitting and walking, but not language. Undoubtedly, the constant colds and ear infections caused some delay, but more than that seemed wrong. Still looking for an answer, I changed her doctor again.

Dr. Troy was a charming, elderly woman from Germany. She was an experienced pediatric specialist who did something no other doctor had done before -- she looked at Valentine. *Really* looked. She measured her head, listened intently to her heart, and then listened again. She examined her facial features, felt her muscle tone, and looked in her ears and at her palms.

"She has a slight heart murmur but it's nothing to be concerned about. She'll probably outgrow it as she gets older. She seems to have a lot of odd features but I'm not sure why. It could be a form of mild Down's syndrome. I'll write a referral for testing at the University Genetics Clinic. Maybe they can figure it out."

Unlike Medicaid, with its uncertain monthly renewals, the University Medical Center issued a permanent plastic card. Registration involved time and paperwork, but it only had to be done once.

The geneticist recorded the size and shape of her head, eyes, ears, mouth, and other features. He looked at her palms and muscle tone as well as birthmarks. Valentine had only one birthmark, a reddened strawberry on the back of her neck.

"I don't think she has Down's syndrome, but I'll do a blood test to make sure," the geneticist said. "You can go back to the waiting room and someone will call you."

By now, Valentine was tired and fussy. When her turn came, she screamed and struggled, so the doctor restrained her on a stiff "papoose" board to draw blood. When the ordeal was over, she clung to me and sobbed.

Weeks later, Dr. Troy received the report. "Her test showed normal female chromosomes. It's not Down's syndrome, but her facial measurements are abnormal. Her head size is small, indicating her brain isn't growing normally, and she is underweight for her age. Try to encourage her to eat more."

Valentine had an excellent appetite but still wasn't growing adequately. To encourage her to put on weight, I began adding extra butter to Valentine's food and instant breakfast mixes to her milk.

Karen came for Valentine's infant stimulation lesson.

"Wow! She's going to get fat if she keeps eating that much." Karen watched Valentine grab food in the palm of her hand.

"And wait until you see her walk," I bragged.

"She *is* walking better," Karen agreed. "But her talking and understanding are still delayed. Does she get speech therapy in school?"

"Yes. It's a good program and her therapist says she's doing well."

Valentine *was doing well*. Alice and Ben sang while the baby tottered around in circles attempting to dance, and they all laughed. They played with her for hours at a time and Valentine, who had previously gone out of her way to avoid eye contact or touching, began watching the children and imitating their games. In spite of all her problems, I enjoyed having a baby in the house again. But I should have known it was too good to last.

"I hardly know Tara anymore. CPS took away a normal child and destroyed her."

Tara's mother

TARA THE TERROR

I came home after getting the kids from their activities and found my husband, Gary, lying on the couch, sweating heavily and complaining of pains in his chest and arm. I called 911 and within minutes an ambulance rushed him to the hospital where he was admitted to the intensive care unit.

That night I tossed and turned in my king-sized waterbed that now felt so empty and lonely without Gary. I didn't fall asleep until well after three in the morning, and then only fitfully. Feeling lost without my husband's reassuring presence I called the hospital several times during the night, but it took until morning for tests to confirm Gary had indeed suffered a heart attack.

I kept remembering how he had looked in the hospital, so helpless in that glaring cardiac intensive care unit with an oxygen tube attached to his nose. Wires taped on his chest were connected to a monitor, beeping steadily as a line showing his heartbeat moved up and down across a screen. A blood pressure cuff attached to his arm took his pressure every few minutes.

The blood pressure cuff irritated Gary's arm and he was relieved when the doctor finally ordered its removal. Soon he had recovered enough to leave intensive care and move into a private room. I knew he was getting better when he began complaining about the "lousy hospital food" and his forced inactivity. Near the end of his hospitalization, Gary asked to see the kids.

Although written hospital policy prohibited children on the floor, the nurses gave me permission to bring them for a short visit. Alice and Ben understood the rules of the hospital and were quiet and well behaved. Valentine smiled and cooed at the nurses. She danced in little toddler circles, which amused the nurses. This friendly little girl brought a ray of sunshine and renewed life to the sober hospital floor.

Gary's recovery was lengthy. He spent ten days in the hospital and remained in bed another six weeks after returning home. I had my hands full caring for him and the children, as well as keeping the house neat and ready for any surprise visits Children's Protective Services might make. This wasn't the time to take on the responsibility of another child. Gary was still bed bound when a CPS caseworker called, trying to place a two and a half year old girl.

"I'm sorry, my husband is sick and I'm only licensed for one child -- I'm at my limit. I really don't think I could handle a two year old at this time."

"I can get you a waiver to allow one more child. She's a wonderful little girl, cute, smart. She really won't be any trouble at all, and I can arrange preschool."

I hesitated.

"I have to find her a place today. I promise, you will love her."

Something's wrong here, I thought. With Gary so sick, I knew it wasn't a good time to take a troubled child.

"Why is she being moved?"

"There were problems with the foster home she was in and she had to be removed this morning. She's sitting in my office right now without any placement. She's been in several different homes and has experienced abuse, but I think your home will be perfect. You'll really love Tara."

Like many foster parents, I'm a soft touch and it's hard for me to turn down any child. But more than that, I knew several different foster parents who'd had trouble getting CPS to place children in their homes after refusing a placement.

Foster parents got together once a month for a local support meeting, and we often discussed placement policies. Children's Protective Services had so many children to place that they pressured families to take more children than they should, and penalized those who refused. I knew families with twenty children.

So, although my better judgment told me not to accept another child, I gave in to the caseworker's desperate high-pressure tactics. A few hours later she brought Tara.

At two and a half years old, Tara was adorable. Her red, Shirley Temple ringlets and splash of freckles across her nose fitted her animated, outgoing personality. She ran about the house bumping into things as she explored every corner. She missed nothing.

"She's a clumsy child and has numerous bruises," the caseworker said as she showed me the marks on Tara's legs.

Tara continued running around the house nonstop. She made herself at home and promptly labeled my Shetland sheepdog "Lassie," a name she still used even after she learned the dog's real name. She called me Mom, Gary was Dad, and she quickly learned Alice and Valentine's names. Ben, who was not much older than Tara, became "that boy."

On Tara's first night, I let the children sit in a circle in the living room while I read stories. Alice and Ben were excited about having a new sister and each insisted on sitting next to her. Circle reading was much easier for me than reading three separate stories and by bedtime I was as tired as the children. They loved this group reading, which we continued on and off for several years as children came and went.

One morning, a few days after joining our family, Tara woke up with marks on her face that looked like cigarette burns. Of course, they were not burns, and unlike burns they were spreading. It was Sunday and the doctor's office was closed so I took Tara to the hospital emergency room.

The doctor examined her and glared at me, "How did this happen?" he asked.

"She's a new foster child," I said. "She woke this

morning with this rash on her face. She was fine yesterday. I'm also concerned how easily she bruises. Can you do tests to find out if there is something wrong?"

The doctor called in a skin specialist who diagnosed the skin problem as impetigo and gave me an ointment for it. I was concerned that it might be contagious but the doctor reassured me that it wasn't. I now suspect it was related to the stress of being moved to yet another new family. It's hard being a foster child. The doctor also did blood tests, which came out normal. He concluded that Tara was a healthy child who ran into things hard enough to bruise herself.

Except for this one incident, Tara seemed fine. She was such a chatterbox – not only verbal, but also bright, active, and cute. At first, I found it hard to understand why this feisty redheaded charmer had been moved to so many different homes.

What an adorable child! I thought as I put her to bed. When I took my shower, I discovered the shampoo was watery and wouldn't foam. Tara had dumped out the shampoo, leaving just a little on the bottom for color, and had filled it with water.

Tara's incessant activity brought a party-like atmosphere to our house and kept me busy non-stop. She was smart, and full of mischievous tricks like this, but also destructive. I think she imagined herself to be Tarzan of the Apes because the curtains in her bedroom became swinging vines until the rods bent under her weight. She was destructive with toys and could break even the sturdiest. She took a fish out of the tank and watched with fascination as it flopped about the floor. I intervened quickly and the fish survived. I couldn't leave Tara out of my sight for an instant.

"No," was a difficult word for Tara to hear. When she couldn't have a demand filled *immediately,* her freckled face turned almost as red as her hair, she stiffened her body and fell straight backward onto the hard ceramic-tile floor where the carpet ended. I grabbed her before she hit the ground.

"It's lucky I caught her," I gasped the first time she fell. "She could have burst her head open."

I soon realized that whenever Tara fell backward, someone was always close enough to catch her. Although she was smart enough not to get seriously hurt, her delicate skin was covered with bruises. To protect myself from abuse charges, which seemed a constant threat to foster parents, I reminded the caseworker about her bruising.

"Yes, I know she hurts herself. She doesn't look where she's going and runs into things. I'm setting up an eye examination for her. After the beating, I think she may need glasses.

"What?" I asked. I hadn't heard about this before and was still new enough at foster care to be surprised.

"The father in one foster home beat her across her head and eyes. She lived there for six months and also in five other homes this year. How is she doing with you?"

"We're having some problems with temper tantrums and she bit Ben once. My kids are upset with her volatile temper and her constant activity is exhausting. My husband's not well, so I'm on my own. I'm feeling overwhelmed."

"Tara has an appointment with a neurologist next week," the caseworker said, "and also a psychologist who might be able to give you some suggestions. The only neurologist who accepts Medicaid is out of town. It's too far for our drivers, so you'll have to take her yourself. Here's information for the doctor," she handed me a manila folder.

The folder contained Tara's history. The beatings to her head had been violent and her arm had been twisted and broken. According to the report, another foster child, a teenaged boy living in the home, had sexually molested Tara.

I'd heard of such things happening but thought they must be rare. Tara 's sexual knowledge far surpassed what any two year old should know, but sexual abuse wasn't the reason Tara was in foster care. The state had taken Tara because her mother was young and homeless. They had no alternative programs to help her mother find a home or learn job skills, so they took the toddler into protective custody and left the teenaged girl in a homeless shelter. All this abuse, along with the behavior problems, happened *after* CPS took Tara into their protective custody.

I took Tara to the neurologist. The bruises on her head

had faded and she had no sign of brain damage. Her reflexes were normal and her intelligence, in spite of emotional problems, appeared above normal.

About this time my mother came to visit for the week. Tara clung to "Grandma," demanding constant attention. She'd had so many Moms in her short life she went to anyone -- she called every woman, "Mom" or "Grandma," and every man, "Dad." However, "Dads" were scary people and Tara kept her distance from them. Tara needed attention like a drowning child needs air and she grasped with an urgency too desperate for any one person to fill. I was grateful having help, but soon my mother became exhausted.

"I came to see my grandkids. That little one demands my full attention every waking moment." "She's still adjusting," I said. "I'm sure she'll calm down in a while."

"She has trouble with changes," Grandma observed. "I think that's related to her temper tantrums."

My mother was right. "Come on Tara, let's get in the car," was enough to start her crying or throwing herself backwards. Getting out of the car caused an equally violent reaction. Getting in an elevator, getting out, walking from one room to another. Any change brought on temper tantrums. Six to ten times an hour Tara turned red, and fell on the floor screaming and kicking her feet. Something had to be done to get this situation under control. I decided to try a behavioral program using a token economy. I'd had success with it before.

I bought a variety of children's party toys and a box of multicolored poker chips. "We're going to have a store," I announced to the children. "You're going to earn tokens to buy things. Alice will get tokens for going to school and getting good grades. Tara and Ben will get tokens for behaving at home. Everyone will get tokens for eating dinner with good manners and brushing their teeth at night. We'll have store time after dinner. You can use your tokens to buy things."

The kids thought a store would be lots of fun, and it was. I made sure every child had some chips every day, enough to buy a small prize or to save for a larger one. During the day, whenever Tara had a tantrum, I calmly ignored the tantrum and pulled a chip out of my pocket for Ben "You're doing such a good job *not* having a tantrum. Here's a token for you!" I exclaimed loudly in Tara's direction. If Ben had a period of pouting, as he occasionally did, Tara earned a chip for *her* good behavior. She also earned chips for staying at the table through dinner and for brushing her teeth. At the end of a few days, Alice and Ben had saved over twenty poker chips, Tara had three Alice and Ben each bought a plastic whistle and were sent outside to blow them. Tara had only enough to buy a plastic spider, the same item she'd bought every day for the past week.

"I don't want anything. I'm saving my tokens," she said, keeping her little face stiff to hold back the tears. She longed for a whistle, too, but for days it seemed out of her grasp.

Finally, the program began working. I went shopping with Ben and Tara. We walked into the store -- no temper tantrum. We walked from aisle to aisle -- no temper tantrum. We stood in line to pay -- no temper tantrum. And finally, we walked out of the store -- no temper tantrum. Tara earned numerous chips, and that night she had enough to buy a whistle. That whistle became her most precious belonging. For days, awake or asleep, Tara kept it locked tightly in her palm.

Soon, the tantrums decreased to mild pouting sessions and dropped to fewer than ten a day. But temper tantrums were only the tip of the iceberg when it came to problems and our honeymoon period was coming to an end. Tara, who had already bitten Ben on occasion, began biting him several times a day. Tara had play therapy once a week but this wasn't enough. The psychologist was pleased to see Tara's decreased tantrums but had trouble giving me any helpful suggestions for dealing with her biting.

"I would usually suggest having the other child bite back, or placing Tabasco sauce on the tongue -- these sometimes work, but since she's a foster child you aren't allowed to do anything punitive. How are you handling it?" the psychologist asked.

"I put her in 'time-out' in her bedroom. It's the only type of discipline CPS allows, but it doesn't work with Tara."

At the psychologist's suggestion, I began taking chips away whenever Tara bit, and this seemed to help -- for a while.

Good-natured Ben continued playing with Tara. Children can be very forgiving. But eventually he started complaining and asking when she would leave, a thought that had also crossed my mind more than once.

"Keep her through the holidays, at least," Gary suggested. "We'll see if things don't smooth out after that."

Christmas came. CPS had presents and a party for the children. I took my kids to the party and Tara sat on Santa Claus's lap. Unlike many two year olds, she showed little fear of strangers. Three year old Ben wasn't sure about all this and watched Santa from the safety of my lap, which he shared with Valentine.

I talked to other foster mothers at the Christmas party. One woman had cared for Tara in her home for a short time the previous year.

"She kicked me in the stomach and I was bleeding internally. I had to be hospitalized, but CPS only pays for the children's medical expenses. I still have medical bills and pain. I only kept her two weeks. There are other parents here who have had her, too. She's on everyone's blacklist. If you hadn't taken her, she probably would have gone to the children's home."

Ruth and Joseph were there with their new foster children. I hadn't seen them since our licensing class. We were too busy adjusting to our new families to have time for socializing.

One of Ruth and Joseph's foster children was a girl named Pixie, who appeared to be about twelve years old. I found out later she had just turned sixteen. Pixie's mother was an alcoholic who had abandoned her at birth.

Pixie had the distinctive eye shape and facial features associated with Fetal Alcohol Syndrome, but this resemblance was subtle and I didn't see it then. It wasn't until a few years later when I saw her baby pictures, that I realized how closely Pixie resembled Valentine.

Pixie played with my children and sat on Santa Claus's lap along with the little ones. I liked Pixie and I think she liked my family.

The kids had fun at the party and Tara was on her best

behavior. But that night, for no reason whatsoever, she bit Ben again -- hard enough to leave a large bruise on his chest.

This was too much. Gary and I agreed this had to stop or Tara would have to be removed from our house. The caseworker who originally placed Tara in my care had quit, so Tara had a new worker.

"Her previous caseworker promised me daycare if I needed it," I told the new worker. "Could you arrange this? We need a break from having Tara around all day. She's too exhausting."

"I can't understand why she would have said that."

"What do you mean?"

"There's no money for daycare this late in the year. But even if there were, Tara has already been kicked out of three daycare centers for biting. No one will keep her because they don't have the staff to watch her closely enough."

Tara bit Ben again and he bit her back this time.

"That boy bit me," she cried.

This seemed to make a difference and her biting stopped. Then it started again -- with a vengeance.

I heard the refrigerator door open for the hundredth time that day. Tara had a ravenous appetite and although she ate everything in sight, she remained thin. All her running around and getting into trouble must have taken a lot of energy.

"You just had a huge breakfast half an hour ago. Wait for lunch," I said.

Frustrated, Tara walked out of the room and a minute later I heard a howl. I found Ben rubbing his shoulder where Tara had bitten him. I separated the kids and put them down for their naps, but Tara didn't sleep. She spent the time in her room removing the window screens and bending them in half. She gained strength with her anger. Later that afternoon she broke the wheels off Valentine's riding toy -- a whistling train all the kids had loved, even Tara. Finally, the day was over. Tara and Alice were asleep in their room, Ben in his, and Valentine in her crib. Asleep, the four looked angelic.

I was getting ready for bed when I heard the scream. Tara had woke up, gone into Ben's room, and bitten him. He came out rubbing his buttocks and showed me teeth marks. I calmed him down, put both children back to bed, and called the CPS emergency number.

"You have to remove Tara in the morning " I said, after explaining the situation.

"Do you want us to come and get her tonight?"

"No, she's asleep now. But I want her out tomorrow."

I slept poorly that night, every wrinkle in the sheet felt like a sharp rock. I had not taken foster children to reject them. Tara had already experienced far too many rejections in her short life and now I was guilty of doing the same thing.

Tara's caseworker called the next morning. "Can't you please keep her six more weeks until we reunite her with her mother?"

"Can't she go back with her mother now?"

"No, but if she can remain stable in one home for six weeks, we think her mother could manage her."

"I want her out today," I said.

"That's difficult but I'll move her as soon as I can find a place," the caseworker promised. "I'll get back with you later."

The next three days Tara continued biting Ben in the back, chest, buttocks, and stomach, and as if this wasn't enough, she began pushing Valentine. The toddler fell on her padded diaper and cried -- more from frustration than injury. Gary was still restricted to bed and complained that Tara gave him chest pains. He was afraid he might have another heart attack from the stress she caused. Alice and Ben wanted her out. Even the dog ran from her tail-pulling attacks. I was exhausted.

The caseworker still couldn't find another home for Tara. I called her daily and felt as though I was begging.

"It's been three days. You have to move her out today. I can't have her hurting my other children. I wish I didn't have to do this," I said while untangling the phone cord Tara had tied into knots.

"You don't. It's not too late to change your mind."

"I'm sorry, but I do. She's hurting my other foster child now as well as my son. I like Tara but we can't live with her, especially with my husband recovering from a heart attack."

"I'll get back to you as soon as I find a placement for her," the caseworker promised. I felt both relief and sorrow when the caseworker moved Tara later that evening.

When foster children leave my home, they leave forever. I rarely hear from them again. It's as though I've never known them. But they never leave my mind, or my heart.

*Low-birth-weight infants are at increased risk
for numerous problems which affect not only
their health but their family interactions.*

BORN TOO SOON

T he first week after Tara left, I had a lot of extra time for Alice, Ben, and of course, Valentine. Naturally, this situation couldn't continue. It's like the "law" which facetiously says, "The time it takes to do a job expands to fill the time available to do it."

Like time, the needs of children also expand. The other children soon took the time I had been devoting to Tara. Alice, now in first grade, began needing daily prompting to do her homework.

"I don't want to do this. It's too easy," she complained.

She was right, it was simple for her, but it sometimes took hours of reminding before she would do the ten-minute assignment. I found my first gray hair and imagined I would turn completely gray from frustration before the school year ended.

Ben, who was not yet school age, *wanted* homework, and I had to make pages of "homework" for him to do too. He delighted in working simple math and reading problems and had already learned to play games on our small computer, a simple model with none of the complicated extras. Although it intimidated me a bit at first, my patient three-year-old son eventually taught me how to use it.

Gary was feeling better and began helping do light

chores around the house. He wasn't ready to return to work yet, but I enjoyed his company and appreciated his help.

Yes, time expands to fill a void -- and when one is a foster parent, so do children. When Tara departed, she left a hole which needed filling, and is soon was. The new baby was striking. His eyes were dark blue and he had long black eye lashes, which gave him the appearance of wearing mascara. Nothing missed his alert gaze as he visually explored the room. He was quick to smile, this little one. He was one of those lucky people, the kind who makes friends effortlessly. A born socialite, he loved everyone and everyone loved him. This was Woodrow Jr. at four months old -- all eight pounds of him.

Woody's mother was in her seventh month of pregnancy when cocaine use caused her to go into premature labor. She had an easy birth but something was wrong with the baby. He had stiff, tight muscles and had trouble moving his arms and legs -- a problem caused by drugs and prematurity.

Woody's tight muscle tone made him difficult to hold and dress. Because of his unyielding arms and legs, and bent feet, I couldn't put pants on him. I dressed him in legless sleepers that tied on the bottom.

"He's wearing a dress Mom," Ben and Alice joked.

When I placed my hands in his palms, Woody's hands locked onto my fingers. He pulled himself into a stand and supported himself on stiff legs. His stiffness later interfered with learning to sit and walk, but for now, he was thoroughly pleased with himself and he smiled and cooed to tell me so.

Woody had stayed in the hospital several weeks before going home with his mother. A short time later, CPS discovered she was still using cocaine and moved him into a shelter home. After a month, his status changed to foster care and he moved into my home. Hospital, mother, shelter, and foster care -- four different living situations in just four months.

Moving from home to home is stressful for children, and it isn't unusual for young infants to get sick as a result. Within twenty-four hours, Woody wasn't smiling anymore. He had become lethargic and irritable, not at all the happy baby he'd been the day before. The doctor's office had closed for the weekend, so I took him to the hospital emergency room. The doctors and nurses knew Woody.

"I took care of him when he was born," one nurse said. "His mother came into the hospital in labor, high on cocaine and stinking drunk. It was the first time in her pregnancy she'd seen a doctor. Woody was a favorite with the nurses in the newborn nursery."

I asked the nurse for a copy of his medical records and she gave me a summary. There had been bleeding in his brain and he had stopped breathing several times. He had numerous other complications related to cocaine exposure and the resulting premature birth.

"This baby had a hard time. It's a miracle he's alive," I said.

"His hospital bill is over a hundred thousand dollars and this is just the beginning," the nurse shook her head and frowned."

The doctor arrived and examined Woody. "He has a bad ear infection. His eardrum is about to rupture from the pressure. I'll start him on an antibiotic right away. Did you know this baby is mentally retarded?"

This surprised me because Woody was such an alert baby and in spite of his restricted movement, he could smile and turn himself over. These were normal activities for a two month old. I subtracted two months from Woody's age to compensate for the prematurity.

"What makes you think so?" I asked.

"See how thick his eyebrows are. They go all the way across his brow. That's quite abnormal in a newborn. Also his ears are low set, another sign of retardation. I'm afraid this baby has numerous small facial abnormalities. I'm sorry, but he's clearly retarded."

I wonder if the doctor would have voiced such an insensitive, and in this case, incorrect diagnosis, had I been his birth mother.

Woody recovered from his ear infection and soon became everyone's favorite baby. Alice loved holding and feeding him. Ben was elated when Woody laughed at his silly antics. Valentine clapped her hands, showing off her newest skill. My kids were pleased that Woody could hold onto a rattle without dropping it. Once he gripped it, someone had to pry his tight fist open to remove it. He sat in his infant seat shaking the rattle and smiling. He made happy cooing sounds, but it was months before he began babbling.

I'm the family worrier and remained concerned about his development. Feeling he would benefit from physical therapy and wanting it started as soon as possible, I asked his CPS caseworker for an evaluation of his tight muscle tone.

The doctor at Children's Hospital who examined Woody was also concerned. "His muscle tone is abnormal and he needs therapy to prevent further delay. I'll talk to Children's Protective Services."

His recommendation was promptly filed and forgotten. There was no money in the foster care system for preventative services.

The doctor's prediction was correct. It took almost a year before Woody could sit well, and he didn't walk until shortly before his second birthday.

The court had put Woody's mother on probation for giving birth to a substance exposed infant. When CPS caught her with cocaine, they called the police and she was put in jail. Luckily, the judge was lenient and released her to a rehabilitation center a few weeks later, where she worked hard breaking her addictions. The promise of being reunited with her newborn son compelled her to break her drug habit, and CPS began allowing regular supervised visits at their office.

Woody's caseworker called. "I can't get a driver today. Would you mind bringing him to the clinic for a visit? You can meet his mother while you're there."

I was surprised to find Woody's mother a pleasant, educated woman, who truly loved her baby. This was not the picture I had gotten from the caseworker or the newspapers, which portrayed drug addicted mothers as cold and uncaring. I began learning how much these mothers suffer when they lose their children. It was easy to forget that these babies have mother who, in spite of their problems, love their children. Woody's mother never missed their visits at the CPS office. She anticipated having him come home soon.

As time went on, Woody began falling behind normal babies his age. He was so stiff that crawling, sitting, and later walking took extreme effort. He rocked on his hands and knees for months before making his first crawling movements. When he sat alone, he was unbending, and his balance so precarious that he fell over sideways like the china doll he resembled. He was not developing age appropriate speech sounds either. I called the caseworker.

"It's been months since his doctor recommended physical and speech therapy. What's the hold-up?"

"All the paperwork is done but we need to find someone to pay the bill. We can't locate any responsible party. He seems to fall through the cracks. I'll get back to you when I learn something."

Eventually, he was assigned an infant stimulation teacher. I requested Karen, who was already working with Valentine.

Valentine loved Woody. She made eye contact with him before ever doing so with adults. When he was in his baby swing, she took tentative toddling steps toward him, touched his hair and talked to him in her own babble language. He smiled, cooed, and squealed in delight at her attention. Alice sang children's nursery rhymes as she danced about the room. Ben, always the clown, practiced jumping as high as he could while making silly faces in an effort to entertain anyone who would glance his way. Woody rewarded everyone with smiles and laughter.

Valentine laughed and her smile at eighteen months was as toothless as Woody's at five months. Because she was so late getting teeth, I took her to a pediatric dentist for a check up.

"I can feel teeth under her gums," he said after examining her. "I think they'll come in on their own. Bring her back in six month when she turns two."

A week later Valentine fell against the corner of a table and cut her upper gum. Soon a tooth began showing through the cut on the middle of her gum line. This was worse than no teeth at all because instead of growing down, the tooth grew straight out. I took her back to the dentist.

"Now we know she has teeth," he said. "The position of the tooth will correct itself."

The medical doctors had more difficulties than the dentist. No matter what they did, Valentine still couldn't get over her cold. Her nose ran constantly, pus drained from her ears, and she was contagious. My children and I were ill far more often than usual that season. Luckily, Gary was cold resistant. Had he gotten sick so soon after his heart attack it could have been serious.

During the next visit, Dr. Troy expressed concern because Valentine's weight had fallen below the fifth percentile on the baby growth chart, making her smaller than 95 out of 100 babies her age.

"She should be growing," I said. "She eats everything in sight and then looks around for more, but she has diarrhea often."

"I'm going to give you some lactase drops to put in her milk. It's possible a milk allergy is slowing her growth."

The lactase drops helped and Valentine had fewer upset stomachs, although she still didn't grow well and her colds continued. So did ours.

Foster parents become accustomed to strangers coming and going at all hours. One day a stranger came to my door. She hadn't called ahead, but just showed up unannounced.

"I'm Valentine's court appointed Guardian. I need to see her. May I come in?"

The Guardian Ad Litem, a volunteer assigned to speak for the child's interest, met Valentine, Alice, Ben, and Woody. She was friendly but I felt uneasy, and judged. She told me about an upcoming court hearing concerning Valentine and said she was not sure whether she would recommend sending her home. She had to determine what the best situation was for Valentine.

The court date came and went. I still had Valentine, but I didn't know what had been decided. The caseworker was in court with several other children that week and unavailable until days later.

"The judge has decided Valentine will stay with you

for now," she said when she finally returned my call. "But she must attend a new preschool program at Sunshine School. The bus driver will call you about the pick-up time."

"Why? She's adjusted so well to Little Bits School where she's getting speech and physical therapy."

"She won't have therapy at Sunshine, but her mother will be going to the program with her. We're trying to teach the mother parenting skills so she can care for Valentine and her other children. When children are taken out of a home for an extended period of time, it's easy for the parents to feel helpless and give up the responsibility of caring for them. Then it's hard for them to get out of this hopelessness and begin handling the day-to-day care. This program is intended to give mothers hands-on training and get them ready to care for their children again.

Unlike Little Bits specialized preschool program, Sunshine was primarily daycare. They kept the children clean, fed, and entertained, but the teachers knew little about caring for disabled children. The goal of this program was reunification between mother and child. In theory, it was an excellent idea, but it was a new program and there were many bugs that needed to be worked out.

The staff was surprised when I came to see the school and told me foster mothers didn't need to visit. They seemed suspicious and uncommunicative. One staff member even asked, "She's not your child so why do you care?"

Valentine's mother seemed to consider me an interloper who had stolen her baby, and the staff at Sunshine supported and encouraged this attitude.

I don't know if Valentine cared about the change in schools. She still showed no sign that she knew me, or anyone else. She went to strangers indiscriminately and continued avoiding eye contact.

The bus driver who picked her up in the morning was often in a sour mood. One day the van arrived with the infant seats removed. Puzzled, I offered the seat from my car -- but the driver refused.

"We're going on a field trip to the zoo and need room to fit the mothers in the van today," she said.

I had to let Valentine go because she was under a court order to attend, but I was furious, and called the school's director.

"You're supposed to teach these mothers good parenting skills. It's not only dangerous but against the law to have babies strapped into adult seat belts."

I later received an apology from the bus driver for her "mistake," but her surliness intensified. Every morning she silently took the baby from me, put her in the seat and left without a word. The afternoon routine was the same in reverse. I couldn't communicate with the bus driver, or the school staff.

Even worse, Valentine's mother started complaining about her care. Soon CPS investigators began showing up at my home at odd hours with ridiculous, but annoying, complaints. Her mother reported that I didn't feed her enough and was beating her. Fortunately, the inspector came at dinnertime and was surprised to see how much such a small child ate. When he opened my refrigerator to see if I had enough food, I invited him to dinner. He politely declined. Valentine had a small bruise on her arm from falling at school. I handed the investigator the incident report from the school that explained how the bruise had occurred. Then I undressed her and handed him the naked baby to show she had no other bruised. She looked up at him, smiled, and tinkled on his suit. By the time he left, the kids had finished eating and my dinner was cold. I resented these intrusions in my life.

Children's Protective Services later investigated me because of Valentine's constant colds, failure to thrive, and diaper rash (there was none). At this time, I was taking her to the doctor at least every other week for ear infections, and doing infant stimulation daily. She was an exhausting, time-consuming child. I spent more time caring for her than I had ever done with my own children, and yet, I was under constant surveillance and questioning from CPS.

"I'm not the abusive mother. We're on the same side -- the child's." I reminded the caseworker.

The children seemed unaware of all this adult brouhaha going on around them. Valentine continued making slow progress. Her walking gradually improved, but she still couldn't understand words. Since understanding must come before speech, Valentine didn't talk. Ben and Alice played and talked to her for hours, but even they began showing frustration over her lack of understanding. She continued avoiding physical contact with adults and disliked being touched, even by the children.

I read a book about an autistic child who rejected all contact with other people. This child improved after being given constant holding and attention, even though he appeared to dislike it at first. Although she wasn't autistic, I wondered if holding Valentine more often could help her get closer to other people in this same way. It was worth a try. I began holding and rocking eighteen-month-old Valentine when giving her a bottle. She hated it and struggled to get way, but I didn't give in this time. Finally hunger won out and Valentine took her bottle in my lap while turning her head and body as far away as possible. After that, I carried, rocked, and hugged her as much as I would a newborn infant. At first she resisted the extra attention, but with continued efforts, she began to accept, if not like it. Eye contact remained fleeting at best. Improvement came slowly.

One morning, the bus driver told me the bus pick-up time would be moved half-an-hour later.

"I won't be home. I drop my own children off at school at that time."

"We've taken more children onto our route and this is Valentine's new pick-up time. I can't be flexible."

I called Valentine's CPS caseworker and explained the conflict. CPS had transport workers for limited doctor visits but not for daily activities such as school. Valentine was attending by court order so she had to go to that school. I thought about driving her, but it was nearly two hours, round-trip.

I was discouraged. After nearly a year in my care Valentine showed no sign that she knew me. Her chronic colds infected my entire family. I had to deal not only with doctors, but also with abuse reports due to her failure to thrive. Was I willing to spend hours each day driving her to this school? Ben, Alice, and Woody all needed my time and attention too. This wouldn't work. CPS would have to make a choice between my home and the school.

I lost, although it was Valentine who really lost.

I felt a mixed sense of sadness and relief as I wiped her runny nose for the last time. Then, as though she knew, she toddled up to me, looked me straight in the eyes and hugged my leg. This was the first, and only time, that Valentine did this.

I left a note with my phone number in Valentine's file and a week after she left I received a call from her new foster mother.

"What did you do about her cold? She's made everyone in my house sick."

I suddenly realized that for the first time since Valentine had entered our life, no one in my family was ill.

But now, with just Alice, Ben, and Woody, the house seemed empty. It was time for another child.

The long-term affects of prenatal exposure to alcohol and other drugs are significantly reduced when parents, teachers and other professionals meet the special needs of substance-exposed children early.

TRIPLE TROUBLE

V alentine was gone, leaving only Woody and my birth children. I was relieved having the recent hassles behind me, but the kids, especially Alice, missed her.

"I wish I had a sister," Alice mourned.

Children's Protective Services was finalizing plans to return Woody to his birth mother. I called CPS placement and told them I had an opening for an infant girl. Six years before I'd had only one baby, Alice, and she had taken all my time. But now I'd become more efficient and after going from four children to three, everything seemed easy. Alice was in school, so I had time to spend with the boys. I savored every last moment I could with Woody.

It was late spring and the weather grew warmer each day. Flowering plants of all kinds were blooming. White, pink, and red blossoms appeared overnight and the sweet honeysuckle fragrance hung heavily in the air. A baby rabbit crossed our path when I took the boys for a walk. The world was renewing itself. It was a time for new life and spectacular growth.

Woody was a handsome baby with a full head of black hair and his eyes were still a deep ocean blue, unchanged from the first day I'd first seen him. They sparkled when Ben played pat-a-cake or peek-a-boo with him. The boys both loved these simple games. Woody knew the games and attempted to play, but he was unable to use both hands at the same time, or bring his hands together. When he used one hand, the other locked into a tight fist against his body. He could reach objects on his left side with his left hand and objects on his right side with his right hand, but couldn't reach across his body or raise his hands to his mouth. Karen, his infant stimulation teacher, showed me how to gently shake his arms to relax both hands at the same time and how to encourage him to reach for an object on the opposite side of his body.

On a typical morning, eight-month-old Woody woke, played happily in his crib, and cooed while I helped Alice get ready for school. Sometimes Ben secretively climbed in with him and I'd find the two boys entertaining each other in whispers. Ben, of course, did all the talking, although Woody added his own baby noises. As soon as Woody saw me, his face lit up with an enormous smile and he let out a squeal. He was a good-natured baby who rarely cried.

Woody always greeted me with such a cheery smile and joyful sparkling eyes that I never resented the extra time he required. To make dressing easier, I chose loose fitting clothes. When I changed his diaper, I massaged and exercised his arms and legs, and I sang in my off-key voice. Woody didn't mind my bad singing.

Woody didn't remain my only baby for long. Valentine had only been gone a week when Sammy arrived. He was a four-day-old cocaine and alcohol exposed infant who came to me from the hospital. I know children that age aren't especially attractive, but to call Sammy "not especially attractive" would have been a compliment. He looked downright ragged. He had a sad, oddly shaped face, and although everything was in the right place, his small droopy eyes were set too far apart and the flattened bridge of his nose made them appear even wider. His flattened upper lip accentuated his dull, unfocused expression. His ears were set low on his head and stuck out. Numerous red marks spotted his eyes and nose and a large rash-like strawberry spread across the back of his neck. This child, whom I later learned had the facial features of Fetal Alcohol Syndrome, was one of the homeliest infants I'd ever seen. Sammy's personality was no better than his looks. He turned his small head and fragile body away from me whenever I held him. I was accustomed to babies like Woody, who smiled and gazed at me in fascination during diapering. We had great conversations about bare toes and bare bottoms. But Sammy turned away and looked at the blank white wall. I'd taken down the bright pictures because when he looked at them, his whole body trembled and he cried. They were too stimulating. I diapered Sammy quietly, without singing or playing with him, while his thin little arms and legs shook as he silently suffered from the effects of drug withdrawal.

Sammy came on a Friday night and like most newborns, he slept much of the time. I slept lightly, listening for his cry. We slept through his first night undisturbed but during his second night the telephone woke me at three in the morning. The call was from a CPS caseworker. She needed immediate placement for a three-month-old infant who'd been abandoned in the hospital the day before. Since the baby wasn't sick and her mother's location was unknown, the hospital had called Children's Protective Services to take her. I never found out why the caseworker waited until the middle of the night to call me. The baby had been there all day and wasn't in any immediate danger.

Having both Woody *and* Sammy put me over my licensed limit of one (which was limited at my request), but the caseworker pleaded that the need for placement was urgent and she would arrange permission for me to take a third infant. I knew CPS planned to reunite Woody with his mother soon, and here was the sister Alice was begging for. I woke Gary and after a brief discussion with him, I called the caseworker back and agreed to take the child on the condition that she take our name off the list of available homes. Although I know some families can do a wonderful job with ten or fifteen children, Gary and I felt we couldn't give adequate time and attention to any more infants. We wanted to make sure our own children, as well as the foster children, grew up in a family -- not an institution.

"I'll be there in an hour," the caseworker promised.

Gary went back to sleep while I prepared the extra crib, chose a sleeper, and made a bottle of formula. Now, there was nothing more to do but wait. I anxiously watched the clock as the hours came and went. I kept busy folding laundry and straightening up. There was always plenty to do with four children, but my mind was on the fifth. What would she look like? How would she act? What new joys and problems would she bring? Morning came, Gary woke first, and soon the children followed. Since it was the weekend, and Gary was off work, he changed diapers and gave bottles while I made breakfast. But even after we finished caring for the children, we were still waiting for my new little one.

Alice was exuberant when she heard that a baby girl would be joining our family. "When will she be here, Mom?" What does she look like? Will she play with me?" She asked question after question.

"You'll have to wait and see," I said. "Her name is Jasmine."

It was almost noon before the caseworker finally brought the baby. Her faded yellow dress was dirty and a size too tight. The cloth diaper she wore was soaking wet. She came with nothing else.

"Here's Jasmine," the caseworker said. The kids couldn't wait to hold their new sister and were soon shaking rattles and playing pat-a-cake with her.

Before she left, the caseworker gave me the baby's history. "Jasmine's mother is a drug addict who left her with a teenaged babysitter but didn't return home," she said. " The babysitter brought Jasmine to her own house and left the baby with her mother, who then gave her to another neighbor. After that the story gets confusing but somehow Jasmine was passed around until someone brought the abandoned infant to the hospital because she wouldn't stop crying."

Jasmine was a pretty baby with large, strikingly beautiful eyes. Her alert, direct gaze sharply contrasted with Sammy's avoidance of eye contact. Seeing Jasmine, Woody, and Sammy together, it was obvious that they all had similar, wide-set eyes. In addition, they each had the same large rash-like strawberry mark on the back of their necks under the hairline. But this was where the similarities ended. Their personalities were quite different. Sammy was sleepy, quiet, and withdrawn. Woody could only be described as "happy-go-lucky," but Jasmine slept little and screamed. Holding her didn't help; she just arched her back and wailed louder.

Alice's excitement over having a sister soon wore thin due to all the crying. "I like Sammy best, even if he is a boy," she said.

Sammy rarely cried. He didn't cry when he was hungry, so I set a timer for each feeding. When I offered him his bottle, he gulped, taking in great gasps of air with the milk. But he could only take the bottle if the room was still and no one talked. He could barely tolerate being held, stiffened, and refused to cuddle. And when he finished his bottle, he slept until I woke him.

As much as Sammy disliked being held, Jasmine loved it. She soon got to know me and stopped crying when I held and rocked her. She wanted me to carry her *all the time.* Any attempt to put her down -- even for a moment -- resulted in a high-pitched screaming cry, as though she were in severe pain. The easiest way to care for Jasmine was to "wear her," so I put her in a cloth infant carrier strapped onto my chest. She fit in the soft carrier, next to my body and was rocked as I went about my daily activities.

As Sammy grew older, he began tolerating being held, but only if I did not rock him, sing, or even talk to him. Like many substance-exposed babies, he liked being held away from my body and rocked vertically in an up and down motion. This was something I learned to do in my foster parents training class. Sammy endured talking when he was in his crib or infant seat, but only if he was facing away from the speaker. He *could* look at people and make eye contact if no one was holding or talking to him. Substance exposed babies are easily overloaded and one experience at a time is all they can handle. It seemed to me that Jasmine cried to close out the world, but Sammy just turned *himself* off.

Although CPS charged Jasmine's mother with abandoning her child and put her in jail for a month, I don't think she ever intended to abandon the baby. I could sympathize with her need for a respite from her endlessly screaming daughter. There was something tragically wrong with both Sammy and Jasmine. It was as though they had been born with limited ability to interact with the world, leaving them unable to give or accept love.

Of course, this wasn't true of all drug-exposed children. Whereas Woody was slow physically, he was quick making friends. He responded to his name, seemed to understand words, laughed easily, and had a friendly, outgoing personality, which attracted many admirers. Wherever I went, people saw my twin stroller and hurried to say "hi" to Woody, hardly noticing Sammy asleep in the other seat, or Jasmine strapped in the carrier on my chest. The clerk at the grocery store deli always had a cookie for Woody. He smiled and cooed his thanks. If I went out without the children, someone almost always stopped me to inquire about "that baby with the blue eyes and charming smile."

Although he had a charming personality, Woody's brain injuries, related to alcohol exposure and prematurity, affected him physically. His muscles remained tight and he was months behind learning to sit up, crawl, and walk. He was nearly a year old before he could open his hands and pick-up or let go of things. Children's Protective Services refused funding for physical therapy so he had to do the best he could without it.

Once a week I took Alice, Ben, and the babies to a nearby park to play. The older kids ran off to play on the swings, Sammy slept in the twin stroller, and I carried Jasmine in the body sling. I formed a depression in the sandbox, which gave Woody enough support to sit and balance himself. He loved sifting the sand through his fingers and this seemed to help him learn to open and close his hands.

I met Ruth in the park with her younger children and we talked. I learned I wasn't the only one having difficulty getting services for my foster children.

"I'm really worried about Pixie," Ruth said, chewing her fingernails to the quick "She needs more psychiatric help than she's getting. In another year she'll turn eighteen and leave foster care. I don't see how she can make it on her own. Her behavior is terribly abnormal."

"She certainly *knows* how to behave. She's a model teenager when she visits in my home," I said. "Pixie is probably just going through a stage. It's normal for girls her age to have difficulty with their mothers. What does she do?"

"She won't clean her room. I don't like her friends -- they're a bad influence on her. We fight all the time. But it's more than that. She's a year behind in school and it's tough for her. I think she has learning disabilities, and she's very immature. She wants to stay a baby. She even walks around the house sucking on a bottle."

"That is odd," I said, offering Jasmine her bottle. "But lots of people do strange things in the privacy of their own home. She acts fine at my house."

"She knows how to put on a good show for outsiders," she paused. "Joseph's worried too."

"I always enjoy Pixie's visits. She's polite and well mannered, and a help with the babies. Alice and Ben adore her. She's welcome to come over any time you need a break. I can always use an extra hand."

Jasmine burped, leaving spit-up all over my arm. "Oh, no. Look at Woody!" I wiped my arm with a cloth. "He has his hands up to his mouth and they're covered with sand."

Although I didn't encourage my children to eat sand, this was progress. Woody had finally learned to bring his hands to his mouth. Tasting is an important way babies learn about their world.

The inevitable had finally come. Woody was going home. Woody's mother had completed an alcohol and drug treatment program along with parenting classes, was holding a job, and living in a safe, clean home. She had been doing well for months. She was pregnant again and CPS wanted to reunite them as quickly as possible so she'd be comfortable with Woody before the new baby was born. I'd become friends with his mother and knew she was ready. She had come a long way. Although caring for five children, three of them infants with special needs was exhausting, I knew giving him up would be hard.

Woody has come a long way in the past six months, I thought, *he'll do great with his mother now.* But I was lying to myself when I thought I was ready to say good-bye. I had known from the start that he would eventually have to leave, but I missed him for a long time.

Fortunately, my remaining babies kept me busy. They were my survival. Woody left, and life continued with him. He had touched us all and even years later, Ben, who was barely three at the time, and Alice, remember him. But life goes on. There was always a baby needing a lap, a cuddle, or a burp. A day rarely passed without a new problem or challenge to face.

One day I was sitting in my big, overstuffed rocking chair with Sammy when his eyes suddenly rolled up into his head and his whole body began shaking.

The child who least deserves it
is the one who needs love the most.

CRY, CRY AGAIN

S ammy's frightening tremors ended as quickly as they began. Since this happened after the doctor's office had closed for the weekend, I would have to take him to the emergency room. Sammy, like most of my substance-exposed babies, often became sick suddenly with problems that couldn't wait until his doctor's regular office hours. Over the past months, the hospital emergency room had become a familiar place. Between the people who had no other place for care, like us, and the real emergencies, it was always crowded. I knew we would wait for hours. Guaranteed. I packed Sammy's bag and we were on our way.

As I expected, it took most of the afternoon before the pediatrician saw Sammy. He examined the baby and took blood samples. It takes a skilled person to get blood from a one-month-old, six-pound baby. The needle he used was so thin it was almost invisible. I was impressed when he got into Sammy's vein on the first try. Even thought the blood was sent with a "stat" order to hurry the testing, it took over an hour for the results to return from the lab.

Before we left, the doctor diagnosed Sammy's problem as tremors due to drug or alcohol withdrawal. He told me not to worry. Sammy had localized tremors in his lips and extremities for weeks after, but he never had another episode as extensive as that first one.

When I arrived home, I found Gary walking the floor with Jasmine, who was screaming inconsolably. I took her in my arms, but she continued crying. She eventually fell asleep exhausted.

"What's been going on?" I asked.

"She's cried like this almost non-stop since you left. I've worn out the floor walking her back and forth, took her for a ride in the car, even swaddled her, but she just screamed and screamed. Nothing calmed her. She just wants you."

"She's been so bad," Alice confirmed. "I missed you Mommy. You were gone too long." Both Ben and Alice wanted to climb into my lap and rock. It had been a hard day for everyone.

Unfortunately, Gary and the kids weren't the only ones who had to put up with Jasmine's temper. Warm weather arrived early and brought a warm, gentle breeze. It was the type of day when one does spring house-cleaning, opening windows and doors to get out the stale winter air and letting in the fresh clean scents of flowers and newly mown grass. Our windows were open, and so were those of our neighbors -- they could hear Jasmine's unending screams. While I waited with Sammy in the emergency room, someone had called Children's Protective Services. Later that afternoon, an abuse investigator from CPS and two police officers arrived.

"We have a report that your baby has been screaming for hours," the CPS investigator said. "What's going on?"

Gary and I explained what had happened.

After the investigator checked Jasmine for bruises and reassured himself that I hadn't been beating her, he apologized and left. His report to CPS was "unfounded."

Like so many other times recently, I felt frustrated and angry. I was beginning to feel that I couldn't handle being a foster mother much longer. The kids were frustrating enough, but the lack of support from the people who entrusted me with these children was disheartening.

Day after day, Jasmine continued her colicky cry. It was tempting to blame such excessive crying on her prenatal exposure to crack cocaine and not look for another problem, but just to make sure, I took her back to the doctor for another check-up.

"There must be something wrong. No healthy baby cries like this all the time," I told the doctor.

He diagnosed a mild ear infection and started her on antibiotics. But even after the ear infection cleared up, Jasmine continued crying in her shrill, high-pitched voice. It seemed to be her way of withdrawing from a world she wasn't ready for yet.

I tried keeping Jasmine at home and away from activity whenever possible. Alice and Ben could stay home with Gary or a babysitter but no one outside my family was willing to watch Jasmine, so I usually saved my errands for her naptime. Gary had a new, less stressful job now, but his heart attack the year before had weakened him and he still needed extra rest. I hesitated leaving the fussy baby with him when she was awake.

Jasmine was six months old before she began tolerating outside activity. She needed to leave the house more often, meet new people and begin learning about the world. We began going on many short outings and Jasmine gradually adjusted to being outside her home. The key to preventing hysterical screaming was to keep the trip short and quiet. She could not tolerate large crowds or noisy places.

I did my best to meet her needs, but avoiding noise and crowds wasn't always possible. One blistering, too hot to cook summer evening, the kids begged to go to a restaurant. Gary was working late, so I decided this was a good idea. I packed extra clothes and bottles for the babies and we were on our way. The diner I chose had fast service and was usually quiet, but that night there was a large, noisy party. It was crowded and the service was slow. Jasmine started wailing and the commotion woke Sammy, who also began crying. I quickly left the restaurant with one screaming infant under each arm. Instead of a sit down restaurant meal, we drove through a fast food pick-up window and took our dinner home in a paper bag. My kids didn't mind and were just as happy with fast food.

At home, Jasmine picked up small bites of hamburger and fries with her chubby fists and shoved them into her mouth. She was quiet as long as her mouth was full but she whimpered between bites. Ben thought this was funny and began laughing and imitating her. Soon everyone, even Jasmine, was laughing along with him. We ended up having a great evening.

Following dinner, I put Jasmine down on the living room carpet to play. She had a unique form of locomotion that I named the "Crab Crawl." She rolled over onto her back, stiffened and arched into a back bend, pushed with her legs, and cried. This moved her forward with the back of her head leading while she faced the ceiling. She moved all around the room this way, arching and crying. When she arrived where she wanted to go, she rolled over onto her stomach, stopped crying, sat up, and began playing. She didn't seem in pain. I think she cried now because it had become a habit and she liked the sound of her own voice. I was never able to find any source for her distress, and she seemed able to turn it on and off at will.

In spite of her crying, I began to love her. She was such a pretty baby and so alert. On the rare occasions when she smiled, her face lit up with such a sweet expression that she looked like an angel. She mastered her developmental milestones at the age listed in the books, if not a little bit sooner, so I knew there was a mental impairment here, and that was a joy.

All in all, the babies brought a great deal of pleasure to my family and me. Everyone had his or her "favorite" and no one lacked for loving attention. However, I found dealing with the "system" nothing but aggravation and headache. The various agencies didn't seem able to communicate with each other or with me. Every group seemed to distrust every other group and this formed an extremely unpleasant atmosphere. Foster parents were quitting faster than new ones could be trained and the same was true of caseworkers. There was an occasion where a previous foster child died in his birth-parents care, and the caseworker who had returned him home was tried for murder. One of the best caseworkers I ever met told me that he was quitting because of this incident.

"This job doesn't pay enough for me to risk my neck," he told me.

The public health nurse from a separate division of CPS came one day to check on Jasmine. I wasn't home so she left a note and returned later in the week.

"I know how busy you are," I said. "I wish you had called first. That would have saved you an unnecessary trip."

"It's our policy to come unannounced. A lot of the mothers wouldn't be home if they knew we were coming. We like to catch people when they aren't expecting us."

"I have nothing to hide and I'm proud to show off how well my babies are doing."

Although I didn't tell the nurse, I resented being treated with the same suspicion reserved for alcoholic and substance abusing mothers.

"How is Jasmine?" the nurse asked.

"She still cries but she's developing well. She's a good eater and is doing everything you'd expect of a six month old. In fact, I think she's even a bit advanced. She already crawls well, tries to pull into a stand, and she knows her name. Jasmine!" I said.

The baby, who was playing with a toy, quickly looked up when she heard her name. She puckered her face as if to cry, then she returned to her toy.

"Her mother has been released from jail, and I expect she'll begin visitations soon," the nurse said. "Can we help you with anything?"

"I do have one problem. I need a babysitter. CPS requires caretakers to be at least eighteen, but they won't help me get an adult sitter, or pay for one either. I really could use a break once in a while. An agency charges more to baby-sit one night than I receive in three days to feed, clothe, and give around the clock care to these children."

"I'm sorry but I can't help," the nurse answered quickly. "Besides, not many people are willing to watch an infant who cries as much as she does."

Jasmine started crying and I tried giving her a bottle. She screamed louder and arched her back in an effort to get away. The nurse left.

The following week, Alice had an all day
family/school outing. It would be a long day and I didn't want
to take the two babies along. This was to be a special day for
Gary and me to spend with just Ben and Alice. They deserved
some special time. Besides, Sammy would get overtired from
being in a crowd, which made his withdrawing worse, and
Jasmine...well you know about Jasmine. I couldn't possibly
consider taking her.

Pixie volunteered to baby-sit. "I could watch the kids at
Mom's house," she said.

I called Ruth and she agreed to Pixie's plan. "Pixie is
seventeen but she's very immature. I'll need to supervise."

I dropped the babies off at Joseph and Ruth's house.
Pixie was excited to have a *real* job, although Ruth was
actually the person in charge.

We had a wonderful day and everyone enjoyed our
time away from Jasmine The Screamer. I felt renewed and had
visions of Ruth and Pixie babysitting during future family
outings. But when we came to get the children, a frazzled Ruth
greeted us. She had sent Pixie to the neighbor's house to calm
down.

"Jasmine never stopped crying the whole day," Ruth
said.

Jasmine looked up and gave me an angelic smile.

Neither Pixie nor Ruth ever agreed to take Jasmine
again. I never did find a babysitter who would watch her twice.

Jasmine soon became an accomplished crawler. She
maneuvered her way around the baby-proofed living room. She
expertly learned to pull herself up and cruise around the
furniture. She'd coo and smile and was the most darling,
chubby faced, dimpled cherub I'd ever seen. She loved to chase
the dog and pull its tail. Our gentle dog quickly learned to stay
out of her reach. She played with toys and explored, but then,
for no reason I could ever discover, she'd roll onto her back,
arch, and begin the "Crab Crawl," crying the whole time. I took
her back to the doctor but he couldn't find anything wrong with
her. She was healthy and developing normally.

Jasmine's caseworker called me "We are making plans
to reunite Jasmine with her mother," she said.

"Has her mother completed drug treatment already?"
"We don't have any proof she uses drugs."
"I don't understand that. You told me Jasmine was a crack baby." (This was when I still used that popular term. I hadn't yet learned the politically correct term: cocaine *exposed* baby. And I didn't know about alcohol).
"The judge wants to send the baby home. I don't agree, but it's out of my hands."
"Will her mother at least have drug screenings?"
"No, she denies using drugs and the judge believes her."
I found this conversation absurd. The baby had clear behaviors of drug exposure and only last week the caseworker had told me that the mother was a known drug addict.
"Does she understand what a difficult child she has? I'm concerned that she might abandon Jasmine again, or even injure her."
"I'm sure everything will be fine," the caseworker tried reassuring me.
There was nothing more to be said. The caseworker didn't like it either, but she had no more control over the situation than I did. Although Jasmine had been in shelter care for three months, she'd never officially entered foster care, so her mother didn't have to complete a performance agreement, parenting classes, or drug testing. Even worse, Jasmine's mother would not have any continuing support services. *What would happen to Jasmine?* I worried.
Before Jasmine left, I decided to have a six months birthday party for her. Earlier in the week, Pixie had helped plan and decorate. She blew up balloons and helped Alice and Ben draw and color a large sign saying "Happy Birthday Jasmine!" The kids were excited. Ruth had a conflict and couldn't make it, but Pixie planned arriving early on her bicycle. My friend, Dianne, was coming too.
On the day of the party, Dianne arrived with her kids but Pixie was missing. I wondered where she was. I knew she'd been looking forward to this day, but she didn't even call.

Anyway, the party was terrific! I baked a big chocolate cake and served half of it decorated with a rattle on top. Everyone sang, "Happy half-birthday to you."

Jasmine knew just what to do with her cake. She took a deep breath and dove in -- head first. She came up, covered with chocolate and looking like a little brown doll. Then she looked as though she didn't know whether to eat the cake or cry, so she did both, crying between bites of cake. Everyone else laughed.

The day was a success and everyone had a great time, although Pixie's absence puzzled me. I called Ruth later and she told me Pixie had been taken to the psychiatric hospital that morning -- something about a temper tantrum that had gotten out of control. Pixie called me a few days later.

"I'm sorry I missed the party," she said. "I'm feeling lots better now and they're letting me out soon. I'm glad because it's really the pits in here."

Soon, Jasmine's going-home day arrived. I dressed her in her prettiest party dress, put matching infant barrettes in her hair, packed her bag, and waited for the caseworker. She played while I took some last movies.

"Jasmine, you're going home with your mother today," I said just as she began puckering-up her face. "What do you think of that?"

Jasmine started crying.

I didn't have much time to miss Jasmine. There was already a newborn waiting to leave the hospital. She'd been born with cocaine in her blood and her mother, who had left the hospital several days earlier, had disappeared.

The key to happiness is learning to stop
and appreciate the little things in life.

FLOWER CHILDREN

W hen a caseworker calls to ask if I have an opening for another child, he gives me a brief description: sex, age, name, and reason the child is being placed into shelter or foster care. After I agree to take the baby, I'm told the worker will bring the child as soon as the paper work is done. This takes four to six hours and the worker usually brings the child to my house at the end of his working day. These few hours of waiting give me some preparation time, but I'm always excited and nervous, and filled with anticipation.

After Jasmine left, I agreed to take the newborn infant, Heather. The waiting was especially difficult this time because I was concerned about getting another screamer. I hadn't asked the caseworker what her temperament was like. He probably didn't know, but even if he had, he wouldn't jeopardize a placement by telling me the baby was difficult. Telling the complete story could make children with serious problems impossible to place.

Luckily, Heather was a sweet natured, happy infant. Heather's teenaged mother was poor, uneducated, homeless, and abusing drugs. She left the tiny infant in the hospital where she'd born and disappeared.

Heather was wearing a miniature hospital nightgown when she arrived. She was six days old and weighed five pounds, the minimum weight required for a newborn to leave the hospital.

A five-pound baby is *small*. She was the size of a half grown kitten. Clothes from Alice's Cabbage Patch doll were too big. Gary could hold her in the palm of his hand. She had trouble finishing one ounce of formula. That was more than her tiny tummy could hold. She needed a bottle once an hour, day and night, and since Sammy still woke up twice a night for his bottle, I was kept busy.

Heather slept in a cradle next to my bed. I took her from the cradle, fed her, and put her back while hardly waking-up myself. Somehow, I survived those sleepless nights and still had enough energy to keep up with Ben and Alice during the day. I think I must have been running on pure adrenalin, happiness, and determination.

Heather was a lovely baby with a pretty, pink face that fit her flowery name. This Lilliputian infant was beautiful. Although small, her features were normal. She appeared perfect. Her muscle tone was excellent for a newborn as she was already holding her head up and looking around. She made good eye contact and loved to be held and played with. Heather was a delightful infant and before long, I began hoping her mother would never return. If she ever became available for adoption, I'd be first on the list. I wanted to keep her forever.

That's not what happened though. The caseworker called me a week later.

"Heather's mother called. She'd been moving and said trying to take care of an infant during the move was impossible, so she left the baby in the hospital. She's ready to take her daughter home now."

"Are you just going to give her Heather?" I asked.

"No, not right away. We need to check out the situation first."

I can't believe you're going to take this baby away and give her to a teenaged drug addict. This is MY baby, tell her mother to GO AWAY. My head was spinning.

It took CPS a week to learn what had happened and arrange the move. The young mother's parents had kicked her out of their home due to her drug abuse and the pregnancy. Her boyfriend's parents said that she and the baby could live with them. The home looked nice and the grandmother seemed competent, so baby Heather went to live with her family. The paternal grandmother was given custody and Heather's mother was placed in outpatient drug treatment.

Heather stayed with me only two weeks. I have nothing left to remind me of her, except one photograph and my memories. That's the way it is with foster children.

Sammy and Ben slept in one bedroom. Alice had her own room and the next child would share it with her. We had to get a girl since CPS doesn't allow children of opposite sexes to sleep in the same room. I had advised CPS about our living situation so I was surprised when they tried placing a developmentally disabled seven-year-old boy with us. Often, either in desperation or carelessness, they call homes that aren't suitable for the child. The placement worker might know a certain home is not the best for a child, but it is better than placing the child in a shelter or temporary receiving home.

I can take a disabled child, but my only bed space is in a room shared with a seven year old girl."

"You'll take a retarded girl?"

"Yes." I had worked with retarded children for many years and felt comfortable with them.

"Okay, someone will call you when we have a child for you."

"Oops, I forgot to remind him, "infants only."

I still had Sammy, of course, and as time went on, I continued worrying about his odd behavior. He persisted in avoiding eye contact, and although he occasionally looked at toys or a rattle, he couldn't follow a moving object. I questioned how well he could see. I also wondered if Sammy heard normally. At times he seemed deaf. He ignored even the loudest sounds and slept through anything. Neither the kid's loud playing nor the vacuum cleaner disturbed his sleep. Nothing -- not even a loud clap, caused him to startle, or even blink --but sometimes he turned his head toward a quiet voice or whisper.

At times Sammy's breathing became forced and raspy. Early one Sunday morning his loud breathing woke me. He was struggling to catch his breath. I took him to the hospital emergency room, hoping the wait wouldn't be too long. No such luck, it took the hospital the usual eight hours to see him. I hated such long waits. Not only were they tedious for me and the baby, but Gary was left watching Alice and Ben. He felt well enough now that he didn't mind, but the kids weren't used to having me gone for so many hours, and they worried that the delay meant something serious had happened to Sammy. I had planned taking the children to the zoo or a park that day, but here I was, stuck in a hospital emergency room while Gary and the kids went without me. Late that afternoon, the doctor sent Sammy home with a decongestant and orders to see his regular doctor in the morning.

I took Sammy to Dr. Soong the next day and he listened to the baby's chest. Dr. Troy, the doctor who had been so helpful with Valentine, had her office across town and required an appointment several weeks ahead. Dr. Soong ran a walk-in clinic just blocks from my home. Although I liked Dr. Troy, convenience and availability won out and I decided to try this new doctor.

"I think he has asthma. Does it run in his family?" he asked.

"I don't know. CPS is still searching for his mother and I don't have any medical history at all."

"When he turns a year old you can give him asthma medicine. For now, I want you to keep giving him the decongestant."

Then, as though it were part of a casual conversation, Dr. Soong asked, "Has he ever turned blue? His heartbeat is too fast. Although he's a month old, it's still the speed of a fetus. It should have slowed down immediately after birth. Let me know if you notice him turning blue."

Sammy had never turned blue but I didn't intend waiting for him to do so either. I called Children's Medical Hospital and arranged an emergency appointment the next week. It was lucky the doctors at CMH could see him so soon. Appointments sometimes take as long as six months to get. However, their doctors are excellent.

Several doctors at the clinic examined Sammy.

"He has a mild heart murmur," one explained. "The valve which is supposed to close at birth is just beginning to close now. If it doesn't shut completely by the time he's a year, we can give him medicine to help. He's all right for the time being."

"I know newborn babies are supposed to sleep a lot," I told the doctor, "but Sammy almost never wakes up. Could this be related to his heart?"

"I don't think that's the problem." His heartbeat is strong. I'm concerned about some other things though. His head is small and abnormally shaped. I want to send him to a neurologist for an evaluation and a CAT scan of his brain."

Before I left, he gave me several appointments with other doctors: a cardiologist, a nutritionist (because his mother hadn't eaten an adequate diet when she was pregnant) and a blood test for venereal disease.

No AIDS test was done because, as it was explained to me, babies don't make any antibodies against AIDS until approximately eighteen months old. A baby whose mother has HIV (the virus responsible for AIDS) will have her antibodies in his body for the first year of life, whether he is infected with the HIV virus or not. Thus, testing an infant for HIV is essentially testing the mother. That is why she would have to sign the permission slip -- although I could sign for any other procedure short of surgery.

The other reason I was given for not doing an HIV test was that the foster parents couldn't sign for any invasive procedure, such as taking blood. This was blatantly untrue. My doctor had taken blood samples from all my foster children as part of their routine health checks. In addition, Sammy had been tested for Syphilis and Valentine for genetic abnormalities through blood tests. It was only HIV testing where I couldn't give my permission.

During his first year I took Sammy to numerous doctors, and although many things were not quite normal, they never found anything seriously wrong. The CAT scan showed that his brain was undeveloped. No one ever told me whether or not this was a normal finding for a two month old, but the doctor didn't seem overly concerned. Eventually the heart valve closed, and his heartbeat slowed to a normal rate.

"He's still small but his growth rate is good," the nutritionist said after his third monthly visit. "I expected 'failure to thrive' but he's doing well. I won't need to see him again."

In spite of his various problems, Sammy was medically stable and improving.

When Sammy was four months old, a public health nurse came to my door unannounced. "I need to check Sammy because he's a crack exposed baby," she said. "I saw him in the hospital and he was almost impossible to feed. The staff propped his bottle against a pillow because he hated being held."

She examined Sammy. "We expected problems but he's doing okay. He's grown and is much more alert than he was as a newborn. He lets you hold him. Many cocaine exposed babies won't tolerate that."

"No, he's not too difficult because he sleeps so much," I said. "But it's frustrating caring for a baby who acts as though he dislikes me. I try holding and talking to him but he doesn't smile or meet my eyes. He's hard to love because he's so withdrawn." I patted Sammy on the back. He'd fallen into a deep sleep the moment I put him in his cradle.

"You're doing a good job with him. Crack exposed babies are *not* very lovable kids. Do you have any questions I might answer?"

"I have very little information about Sammy. Do you know anything about his history?"

The nurse supplemented the information that the caseworker had given me.

"Sammy is a second generation foster child. His mother was raised in foster care herself," she began. "This type of scenario is not uncommon. Imagine what it would be like to be a child growing up in foster care, moving from home to home and feeling that nobody wants you, not even your own parents. Children who grow up in foster care often have low self-esteem and grow up to be adults with serious problems such as drug-abuse, homelessness, and emotional disorders. All these problems seem to tie into each other. There are families who have been raised in foster care for several generations. The state doesn't make a very good parent, and foster kids generally grown up lacking basic parenting skills. Foster care is a 'band-aid ' treatment -- it only hides the wounds. Sammy's mother is an IV drug user and a prostitute. We think she's living on the streets. Sammy is her fifth drug-affected infant. Her other children are all in foster or adoptive homes. His mother wanted to keep Sammy, but when the hospital authorities took the baby away, she disappeared. CPS is still searching for her."

The nurse's visit reassured me that I was doing the best I could with this baby, and I was glad to have the additional information.

Alice and Ben didn't care if their new brother didn't smile or look at them, they adored having a "real live" baby. But for me, Sammy was a *frustrating* child. I hit a low point one day when he was about six months old. He was just beginning to stay awake for a few hours at a time so I took advantage of this by carrying him around the house, talking, and singing to him. No matter how hard I tried to get him to cuddle, or look at me while in my arms, Sammy turned his head and rolled his eyes to escape. I began feeling as though, through his behavior, he was trying to say, "I hate you."

I felt so helpless I nearly called his caseworker and asked her to remove this unlovable child. The only thing that held me back was the realization that moving Sammy, and forcing him to start over with a new family, would only make his unresponsive behavior worse. I knew that all babies, and especially drug-exposed children who have trouble relating to other people, need a stable environment with one consistent caretaker. Children can't develop normally when they're constantly moved from one home to another.

No, this is Sammy's home, I decided, *and this is where he will stay.*

In spite of his problems, or maybe because of them, my little friend, Pixie, took a special liking to Sammy. She often came to visit and help "babysit" while I was home. She seemed reliable under my close supervision, but Ruth warned me *never* to trust Pixie alone with the baby and I knew from my CPS training that abused children could easily become abusive themselves. Pixie had told me her mother was an alcoholic who had abandoned her at birth. Besides both being foster children, Pixie and Sammy shared the same unusual eye shape and facial features associated with Fetal Alcohol Syndrome. Pixie soon developed a special kindred with this poor, homely baby. Perhaps she saw herself in him. She visited frequently.

I remember Pixie sitting at my kitchen table, feeding and rocking the baby while she told me about her boyfriend and her volunteer job working with animals. She had plans for getting her driver's license, finishing high school, and going to college where she wanted to study veterinary medicine. Her eighteenth birthday was coming up soon. She'd been in foster care all her life and was excited about being old enough to finally get out on her own. She also told me that someday she would go to the state psychiatric hospital.

"Why?" I asked, puzzled.

"That's where I'll probably end up. Ruth thinks I'm crazy and so does CPS! She exclaimed.

"You don't seem crazy to me."

I later found out that the state hospital was a placement for only the most seriously impaired mentally ill patients -- those who couldn't be managed in short term hospitals or the community. I couldn't imagine this ever being a place for Pixie -- not then.

"You're listed here as having an opening for a little girl. Is that right? Will you take a six year old?" the voice on the phone asked.

"Tell me about her."

"She's six years old, but about the size of a four year old. She's developmentally delayed and is still in diapers. Her name is Rosey."

"I know Rosey. I met her and her at the children's Christmas party last December. Let me talk to my husband and kids. I'll get back with you."

Rosey was precious, but I knew that she would be a challenge and I'd need Gary's help and commitment. I also wanted to check with Alice before obligating ourselves. She hadn't minded sharing her room with the babies, but Rosey was a different matter. We all needed time to think about this before giving CPS an answer. The caseworker told me Rosey had failed in several homes and I knew that wouldn't make her any easier, but after thinking it over carefully, none of us could say no to that sweet little girl.

The first thing everyone noticed about Rosey was how thin she was -- you could count her ribs from the back. She was an odd looking child. Her head was small and her features pinched. Tiny and fragile, she always seemed sick with one thing or another. She had a long scar on her chest from heart surgery. Rosey's voice was whiny, but she was funny and good-natured. Although diminutive, she loved to eat!

"Gimme cereal. Gimme milk. Mommy. Gimme that. Gimme apple. Mommy. Rosey want," she kept up a constant patter in her high pitched, whining voice. She called me Mommy, but she knew her real mother and missed her.

"Rosey, say, I want milk," I told her.

At first she had difficulty putting three words together, but she soon began imitating me, and later learned to do it herself.

"She didn't talk at all a year ago when she went into foster care," her caseworker said. "If you need anything at all, don't hesitate to call me. Here is my home number."

I was pleasantly surprised. All the caseworkers I'd encountered up to now had unlisted telephone numbers. I don't know if she realized how much her availability meant to me, and how much easier it made my job.

"She's too severely delayed to toilet train," the caseworker continued. "No one's been able to do it. The school bus will pick her up at your house. She goes to Washington Public School. It's a special school for mentally and emotionally disabled children."

Pixie knew about Washington. "That's not a bad school," she said. "I went there."

Washington was an excellent school and Rosey loved it. There were six children in her class and an aide to help the teacher. Each morning I dressed her in a pretty dress with thick lining and slips that hid her painful thinness. She carried her backpack, which contained diapers and a change of clothes.

"Why isn't she toilet trained yet?" her teacher asked. "All the other children in my class use the toilet and I think she's able to learn."

"I'll give it a try," I said. "She'll use the toilet if someone takes her. She just doesn't stay dry in-between."

I started toilet training Saturday morning and was prepared with a dozen pairs of lacy underpants and a box of Rosey's favorite cereal. I took her diaper off and put on a dry pair of pants.

"Dry Rosey," I said, and gave her a bite of cereal I set the oven timer and rewarded her every ten minutes for being dry. When she wet two hours later, I told her, "Icky wet," and changed her pants before giving her a reward for being dry. She liked the lacy new underpants and soon caught on. Ben thought this was a fun game and insisted on a treat for his dry pants whenever Rosey got one. I think he helped train her as much as I did. By Sunday night, I had reduced the "dry pants check" to every other hour. Her schoolteacher continued occasional "dry pants checks" for the next week. Soon Rosey remained dry during the day, but continued needing a diaper at night, as she not only wet but soiled herself in her sleep. When this happened, she took the diaper off and smeared feces over herself and the bed.

"That's an improvement from the last house she was in where she smeared it on the walls every night and ate it," the caseworker said.

I imagine that's why she had to move from her last home, I thought. *Not may people would put up with that kind of behavior from a six year old.*

Rosey continued taking her diaper off and having "accidents." Soon, even with a plastic covering, the mattress was ruined.

Oblivious to the problems she caused, Rosey was a happy and outgoing little elf. She would take off her socks and count her toes, "one, three, two, nineteen!"

She eyed the pile of freshly washed clothes I was folding and pointed to her bright flowered dress.

"Rosey need...that dress! Pretty."

After I dressed her, she laughed and danced around the room. Every bone stuck out. Her knees protruded and her movements were stiff and clumsy. She fell often, but in her pretty new dress, Rosey danced like Cinderella at the ball.

"Rosey pretty!" she said.

Rosey was always the first one to wake in the morning, cheerful and ready for school. At first I had to completely dress her, but soon I began teaching her to dress herself. I used a technique called backwards chaining which I learned while working with developmentally delayed children in group homes. We started with undressing and I did all but the last step, which Rosey had to do herself. I took her nightgown off as far as her ears. She merely had to lift it off the top of her head. Rosey pulled the nightgown off and I helped her dress. Each day I did a little less and Rosey finished the job, starting a little closer to the beginning. Within a month she could not only undress, but completely dress herself as well. I only had to get her clothes out of the closet, which she refused to get near, and tie her shoes. Then she'd get her book bag and dance until the school bus came.

Rosey received speech therapy in school and I continued encouraging longer sentences at home. "I want milk," became "Mommy, I want milk," and finally "Mommy, I want milk, please." Five words! Every day she could say more than the day before.

Halloween arrived, and dressed in a pumpkin outfit, Rosey told me a story. "Mommy, there ghost over there," she pointed into the next room. Then, scrunching up her funny little face, in an attempt to look scary, Rosey continued. "Ghost say roar, roar, roar," she shook her hands up and down. "Ghost get me, oh, no!" her eyes were wide in mock fear. I gave Rosey a big hug. What a wonderful story from a little girl who could barely talk six weeks earlier.

Not everyone in our family was pleased with Rosey. Ben took an active dislike for her. "She's so stupid Mom, " she complained. "When is she going home?"

"As soon as her mommy learns how to take care of her. She's trying as hard as she can."

"You're stupid, Rosey," Ben often told the little girl.

I don't know if Rosey understood, but *I* didn't like it.

"It's not nice to call people stupid," I explained to my four-year-old son. "Rosey is developmentally delayed, so she can't help it when she had trouble learning."

"You're developmentally delayed, Rosey," Ben informed her when he thought I wasn't listening. "Do you know what that means? It means *you're stupid*!"

Not long after that, Ben came to me in tears. "Rosey called me stupid." He learned his lesson and stopped calling her names, but he never liked her.

Rosey ignored Ben. If left to herself, she would climb into her bed, pull the covers over her head, and rock. She also rocked whenever she sat in a chair or in the car. She rocked in long smooth movements and hit her head so often she wore a bald spot on the back. Telling her to stop didn't work so in an attempt to stop it, I invented a game, which we played whenever we were in the car, and she began rocking.

"Rock, rock, rock STOP!" I said, holding her still with one arm on the STOP.

She laughed and stopped rocking for a moment. Soon she learned to stop rocking whenever I said, "STOP!"

At night, when she was in bed, I could hear her playing the game by herself, saying "Rock, rock, STOP!" Still, she would rock her bed from one end of the room to the other, and Alice, who had to share her room, was greatly annoyed.

Rosey had temper tantrums too. Fall on the floor, kick your feet and scream type of tantrums. It took her awhile, but she eventually learned such behavior didn't accomplish anything. Whenever she acted this way, everyone calmly left the room. It's no fun having tantrums if there's no audience.

Rosey's behavior eventually improved enough to take her to a restaurant with the other children. When her food came, she ate three bites of spaghetti before deciding she wanted something else instead. She often did this at home and because she was so skinny, I gave in to her demands. I hadn't realized how much I'd spoiled her and now it had become a bad habit. With much encouraging, Rosey eventually ate the food on her plate.

"Rosey go bathroom," she announced loudly.

The bathroom stall was built with tiles that started at the top of the ceiling and continued to the floor. The stall was not only completely closed in like a box, but small and poorly lit. When I tried taking her into it, Rosey turned pale and began crying. I had never seen her so frightened before.

"No go there!" NO!" she screamed in panic.

I was stunned. What had happened to her? Why was she so terrified?

My heart is in my home,
and that is where I want to be.

A CHRISTMAS WISH

S ammy was six months old when his breakthrough finally
occurred. Previously unresponsive to both people and
environment, Sammy had always given the impression
of being severely delayed. But now he began smiling and along
with that smile, everything about him began changing. He
started looking a people and he stayed awake for hours at a
time, watching, listening, aware of everything going on around
him. At the same time, his tremors decreased and he began
crying when he needed attention.

It may seem that a baby who rarely cries would be
wonderful. It isn't. When he was a newborn, I had to watch
Sammy constantly and keep his bassinet next to my bed so I
could hear every stir he made. I couldn't depend on him to cry
and alert me when he was hungry, wet, or uncomfortable, as a
normal baby does. Learning to cry was an important step in his
ability to communicate.

Now Sammy started advancing with the speed of an
Olympic runner bounding over hurdles along the track. Almost
overnight he began watching the children, and me with his eyes
following us as we walked across the room. He learned to roll
over and rock on his hands and knees in preparation for
crawling. He still didn't babble or make the usual baby noises
children his age normally did but in every other area he made
rapid progress.

By the time Sammy was eight month old he'd come from being almost totally unresponsive to an active, participating member of our family. He sat in his high chair during dinner and ate small bites of table food, which he picked up awkwardly between his fingers and palm. He laughed at Alice and Ben when they made silly faces and they were delighted. Like Pinocchio, the wooden puppet had finally become a real boy.

———————

The long Indian summer came to an end. The days grew shorter and trees turned fiery colors in their final losing battle with the onset of winter. As the weather changed, the season's first chill embraced the morning air. I was glad to see the hot summer days end, but my feelings were ambiguous. I'm never one to welcome the freezing cold and dark days that signal the culmination of another year.

Thanksgiving vacation passed and the children returned to school. By now, Rosey dressed herself every morning. She had to wear slacks to keep warm. Her legs were so painfully thin they'd have frozen in a minute without protection, but she wanted to wear a dress also. Although she looked silly wearing both, she was warm and happy.

Shortly before lunch, the school nurse called, "Rosey is in my office. Her lips have been blue for over half-an-hour. Can you pick her up and take her to the hospital?"

By the time I arrived, the blue tinge in her lips was barely noticeable and before we arrived at the emergency room, her color had returned to normal. I told the doctor as much of her history as I knew. "She was born with a heart problem, a narrowing of a valve, and she had a long scar on her chest where they operated."

"Next time this happens," the doctor said, "call an ambulance so the paramedics can evaluate her immediately. She seems fine now."

Winter was approaching fast. One chilly Saturday morning the kids were home from school, playing inside, watching cartoons and just lazily wasting the day away. Rosey came to tell me something and her lips were a dark gray-blue color. She played as usual and showed no sign of distress while I waited for the ambulance.

When the paramedics arrived, they pasted electrodes on Rosey's chest. Ben and Alice sat quietly and watched from the far end of the room. They had seen ambulances on television and were fascinated by the real life paramedics. Soon Rosey's skin color returned to normal and the heart monitor also read normal, but the paramedics stayed another half-hour to make sure she was stable. They couldn't figure out why she had suddenly turned blue and told me to follow up at Children's Medical Hospital (CMH).

A week later, CMH saw Rosey at the next "heart clinic." Different specialists practice in the clinic and the pediatric cardiologists use the CMH building to see heart patients only one day every three months, so we were fortunate Rosey was able to get an appointment as quickly as she did. During the clinical evaluation she was given several heart tests.

The doctor wasn't sure how serious her heart problem was and wanted to do another test. "I'm going to recommend a holter monitor test for Rosey. A technician will come to your house next week to put a portable monitor on her, which she will need to wear for twenty-four hours while you keep a diary of her activities.

"Would Friday after school be all right? It's better not to have her wear it during a school day because the other children might damage it," he said. "Remember, keeping the diary is extremely important."

The next day the caseworker called to find out how the appointment had gone and told me about plans for Rosey's visit with her mother.

"Her mom is doing so well I have scheduled a visit at her house next Saturday."

"Rosey will be wearing the holter monitor Saturday and someone has to keep a written dairy of all her activities that day. Do you think her mother can do that?"

"I'll talk to her about it."

"While I have you on the phone, I have a question. Rosey seems terrified of closed places like a closet or small bathroom. Do you have any idea why she might act like this?"

"I don't know for sure." The caseworker hesitated. "But I suspect it might be because when she did something her parents didn't like, they locked her in a closet or car trunk."

I was speechless. I could never get used to the kind of horrors these children suffered. Now she was about to spend the day unsupervised with this family and I was helpless to do anything about it.

"Call me next Saturday, and let me know how she did with the monitor," the caseworker said. "You have my home number."

Friday afternoon a technician brought the holter monitor to my house. The monitor was a small box, placed in a cloth carrier, which hung around Rosey's neck and was turned backwards so she couldn't pull it off. Wire leads from the monitor were placed on Rosey's chest with round, band-aid like patches. This contraption didn't bother her and she soon forgot it.

I started a diary of her activities"

4:00 Started monitor. Rosey sitting quietly.

4:05 dancing.

4:15 rocking back and forth violently on chair.

4:25 watching T.V.

4:30 walking around.

4:35 rocking and singing.

4:45 crying.

4:50 rocking in bed

5:00 eating supper.

This was a typical hour in Rosey's life.

Rosey spent the next day visiting her mother and siblings. She had a wonderful time and when she came home she told me all about it.

"Rosey see Joey. Rosey, Joey play. Rosey see Mommy. Rosey see Baby. Rosey want to go home."

She talked for hours, mostly about going home.

Rosey's mother didn't make any entries in the activities diary at all.

"I explained the monitor to her mother," the caseworker said, "and she replied 'of course, she always turns blue when she's cold. I just put another sweater on her and then she's fine'."

So much for communicating. How much time and expense could have been saved if someone had talked to her mother sooner? Again, lack of communication seemed to be a weak link in the foster care system.

After that, I always put two sweaters on Rosey and she never turned blue in my care again.

The caseworker called often and kept me closely informed about the plans for sending Rosey home. I appreciated this consideration, which was rare among CPS caseworkers.

"Rosey's mother doesn't drive," the caseworker said, "so I have set up an appointment at Children's Hospital with an immunologist before Rosey leaves foster care. We want to find out why she is sick so often. The hospital is about an hour's drive from your home. I'll send you a map."

I received the map along with the date and appointment time. The hospital was in another town and I was unfamiliar with the one-way streets, unexpected dead-ends, and roads closed for repairs. In spite of the map, I had to stop twice to ask directions before arriving.

Rosey was excited about going somewhere new. While walking up the long sidewalk to the hospital, she waved and said "Hi!" to everyone we passed. She would have hugged them if I hadn't stopped her. Rosey loved hugging, but needed to learn socially acceptable boundaries.

"Where is the Immunology Clinic?" I asked the volunteer at the Information Desk.

"I d think we have one today."

"I have an appointment card right here. Today is November twenty-sixth, isn't it?"

"You have the right day. I'll call upstairs and find out."

After a brief call she sent me upstairs to wait.

Approximately an hour after we arrived, the clerk at the desk called my name.

"Mrs. Falkner, who are you waiting for?"

"The Immunology Clinic. I'm here with Rosey."

"This is the Genetics Clinic. The Immunology Clinic isn't until next month."

After driving home through the maze of turning and twisting one-way streets, I called the caseworker and told her what had happened.

"It must have been my mistake. I probably gave you another child's appointment date. I've been so overloaded with work that I don't know what's up and down anymore. I won't ask you to drive again. I'll get a CPS driver to take her next time."

I didn't like letting the CPS drivers take my children to doctor's appointments. The driver knew nothing about the child, could give no history, or even accurately tell the doctor what the problem was. For the child to get effective help from a doctor, I needed to be there. The few times I sent a child with a driver, communications were so confused that I ended up having to call the doctor and straighten things out over the phone.

Another reason I was reluctant to allow the CPS drivers to transport my children was because there were to many I didn't trust. Not all, or course. Some did their job well and professionally. However, more than one didn't understand that a baby *must* sit *backwards* in the infant seat to protect it from whiplash if the car stops suddenly. Although Rosey wasn't a baby, most of my foster children were. An infant under six months old doesn't have neck muscles strong enough to support the head during a sudden stop. I was even more disturbed after I explained this and the drivers continued placing my infants facing forward "so they could see better." I began taking my babies to the car and adjusting the seat before the driver had a chance to protest. Whenever possible, I avoided letting anyone besides me or Gary drive my children. While they lived with me -- whether for a week or a year -- each foster child became mine, and they were as precious to me as Alice and Ben.

Not surprisingly, the Immunology Clinic appointment took several months to reschedule and Rosey had gone home by then.

November turned into December and Christmas was everywhere -- trees, Santa Claus, the first flurries of snow. While other children were thinking of Santa Claus and presents, Rosey had a special wish.

"Rosey go home Christmas. Rosey see Mommy, Daddy, Joey, Baby. Rosey live home."

The caseworker knew about Rosey's wish. So did the judge presiding over the case. The new baby, who had been born after the other children were placed into foster care, had been left in the home and was thriving, and the parents had completed their performance agreement. It was time to reunite the family, at least on a trial basis. Two weeks before Christmas, the children started going home one at a time. In spite of the cute things she sometimes did and her rapid progress, Rosey still required constant, exhausting care, and that's why the caseworker decided to send her home last.

I'd been told when I first got Rosey that she'd probably be returning home by Christmas, so I'd been prepared from the beginning. I hoped her mother could make it work out this time, although I had no delusions about how difficult it was to care for a severely disabled child. All of us were ready to see her leave. She had so many problems that she hadn't ever fit comfortably into the family and my kids still didn't like her. They were as happy as she was to say goodbye when it was Rosey's turn to go home.

Rosey was the happiest of all. It was the morning before Christmas Eve and she was dancing in her favorite flowered dress with the full ruffled slip when the caseworker arrived. Holding her beloved backpack, Rosey quickly climbed into the caseworker's car and waved goodbye. My little elf got her Christmas wish.

Don't only see me physically,
but look into my heart. Help me to be
the person I want to be.

SPRINGTIME

It's always a long wait for the winter holidays, then before you know it, they're over and life resumes it's normal, everyday routine. Alice returned to school and Ben entered preschool. They were not the only ones being educated that semester -- Sammy's caseworker told me about a special school for substance-exposed babies.

I called the director to inquire about this program and was invited to tour the facilities. The program was in a basement that the church no longer used. Unlike many preschools in churches, which rent space only for the weekdays, the teachers didn't have to lock up or take equipment home every Friday and return it on Monday. This freed them to purchase better equipment for the children. Unlike the walls of many preschools, which are painted in bright colors and cartoon pictures, the walls in this school were painted in quiet pastel shades. The floors and walls in the infant room were carpeted to reduce noise and the director proudly pointed out the special acoustical ceiling tiles, which also helped absorb sounds. Including the staff, volunteer seniors from the foster grandparents program, and community volunteers, there were nearly as many adults as children in each room. The volunteers talked softly or sang to the children as they played with them. Even though it seemed like play, there was serious learning going on. There was a physical therapy room filled with specialized equipment and unlike most schools, which designate only a corner or a stairwell to a part-time speech teacher, this school had a full time speech and language therapist with her own room. A high priority was put on individualized and small group therapy because many substance-exposed children are delayed in speech and language development.

Sammy was lucky to be enrolled at this time because the school was new and the classes weren't full yet. A month later there was a long waiting list. Children's Protective Services had already evaluated Sammy and diagnosed him as an "at risk" child. Besides myself, the multidisciplinary or M-team included his caseworker, psychologist, social worker, and speech therapist. The professionals on his M-team thought Sammy might have learning problems or developmental and cognitive delays. Being a prenatally alcohol and drug-exposed "at risk" infant also made him eligible for this excellent educational program.

During the tour I was surprised to find my previous foster child, Valentine, in the two-year-old room. Her hair had grown and darkened. It was wavier than I remembered and was arranged in pigtails. When she smiled I could see her new front teeth. However, I was saddened to learn she hadn't made much progress since leaving my home. She was still tiny and hadn't grown much. Her nose was running and the teacher kept tissues nearby to wipe it. She still didn't talk or respond to sounds. From her lack of response, I suspected her mild hearing loss had become worse.

"She's been moved from home to home because of her chronic colds and crying through the night," the director said.

"She never cried during the night at my house. That started after she left my care."

"CPS has moved her as often as once a week. One foster mother took her to the hospital to have her tonsils and adenoids removed and then refused to take her back after the surgery."

It seemed, with the exception of her birth mother, who wasn't allowed to have her, no one wanted Valentine. Some states have programs that give the mother's intensive help to keep their children at home. Unfortunately, there were no such programs available to Valentine's mother at this time. Thus, Valentine was a foster child being bounced from home to home. It didn't surprise me when she didn't recognize me. After finding out what had happened to her, I made an impossible promise to myself. I would never again have a child removed from my home. No matter how difficult the situation seemed, I would do my best to work through the problems, instead of giving up on the child. I was inexperienced and hopeful, and I didn't yet understand that there are some promises that just can't be kept. But I was about to learn.

A child develops trust in others and
reliance on himself through a strong, healthy,
and loving connection with his parents.

LITTLE NO-NAME

The tiny girl clung to the caseworker's leg and peered out from behind her skirt. The child's eyes were large and black and there was an unusually wide spread between them. Her arms were sticks with a knob at the elbow and she reminded me of the photos of starving children in Africa. Even before the caseworker told me, I knew she was a substance-exposed baby. I'd seen enough of these "drug children" by now to recognize the characteristic features.

This child had that same distinctive look I'd seen so often in other substance exposed children. At the time I thought cocaine caused it, but when I later learned at a conference that cocaine exposed babies can't be identified from their facial features, I was puzzled. I had never once questioned my observation that these babies looked abnormal -- about half the children in Sammy's class, including him, had similar unusual features.

"How can you say cocaine doesn't cause any facial abnormalities?" I asked the speaker. "I've seen that same face among cocaine exposed babies. You even had a slide showing a child with those same features."

"That child has Fetal Alcohol Syndrome in addition to the cocaine exposure. Addicted mothers often use several different drugs, which is why we prefer to call the children 'substance exposed', rather than trying to name the numerous possible drugs. Unlike cocaine, alcohol, which is also a drug, *does* cause facial abnormalities. It also causes mental retardation, which doesn't happen with either cocaine or heroin."

I'd never heard this before and was surprised. I'd always assumed illegal drugs would be much worse for a fetus than alcohol.

"Alcohol is such an accepted part of our society I never really thought about how many problems it causes," I said.

"Many people don't even think of alcohol as a drug. But more children are born mentally retarded from alcohol than from any other single cause in this country. Prenatal alcohol exposure can also cause learning problems and hyperactivity as well as serious emotional and behavioral problems. Most of these children have difficulty understanding cause and effect. They have trouble learning from their experiences and tend to repeat the same mistakes over and over."

This was new and disturbing information to me. The newspaper reports about cocaine exposed babies never mentioned alcohol. I didn't know anything at all about Fetal Alcohol Syndrome when the caseworker brought that new little girl.

The caseworker and I talked briefly while the child maintained her lock on the woman's leg.

"She's so small and she has that 'drug look' like Sammy. What did her mother take?" I asked.

"Alcohol, prescription, and street drugs. Anything she could get. Of course, she smoked cigarettes, too. She never did anything to have a healthy baby."

The caseworker brought a battered box containing the girl's clothes from her last foster home. They were old, dingy, and smelled musty from being stored in a drawer too long. Foster parents often buy nice clothes for the children to wear in their homes, but with only the small monthly stipend CPS gives to partially cover the children's needs, it's financially impossible for most foster families to buy a complete new wardrobe for each child entering their home, especially for young ones who grow so quickly. Consequently, the nicest clothes are kept behind for the next child's use. I kept a wardrobe of girl's and boy's clothes sized birth through eighteen months, but I always tried to send a few nice outfits along when a child left my care.

Although this girl was small, she was almost three years old and I didn't have much in her size. I found a few of Alice's outgrown playsuits which she could wear until I was able to take her shopping.

I talked to the caseworker, read the sketchy file, and called the previous foster mother. In this way, I pieced together the child's history as best I could.

The baby had been born several months early. The mother went into labor following a car accident while she was driving drunk. Surprisingly, the diminutive infant survived not only her premature birth, but also drug withdrawal. Many infants in her situation do not.

When she was strong enough to leave the hospital, the mother, who had not yet named her daughter, either refused to sign release papers for adoption, or maybe CPS couldn't find her. The caseworker wasn't clear about this point. She did know that the baby went into foster care under the name used in the hospital: Baby Girl.

Baby Girl was placed in four different foster homes during her first year-and-a-half of life. In her fourth home, Baby Girl, as she was still called, was kept restrained in an infant seat in front of the television all day. She was fed, changed, kept warm and clean, but otherwise ignored. The house was clean and the children were safe. This placement met all the conditions CPS required of a "good" foster home. When she was two years old, the family went on a short vacation. Rather than taking the child along, Baby Girl was moved again.

In her next home, Baby Girl had more freedom to move around and began walking, but she remained shaky and her coordination was poor. Over time, she learned to say a few words.

I visited her previous foster family. "I'm the only one who can understand her speech," the foster mother told me. "She hits other children but doesn't play."

I observed that the older children in the home watched the younger ones and kept them out of trouble. They took the toys away and kept the babies sitting quietly in front of the television. Children's Protective Services forbids corporal punishment and recommends disciplining children with time-out or behavioral modification instead. Spankings are useless on foster children, who have learned to ignore anything less than the severe beatings that led them to be taken from their parents, and placed into foster care. But this family had other ideas for discipline, and the few privileges the older children had were taken away if they messed up the house. Long writing assignments, such as copying chapters out of the Bible, were also used as punishment. The foster home had fifteen children and the housekeeping was immaculate. CPS was pleased -- this was their idea of a model house.

"Baby Girl is such a fearful child. She's terrified of anything new. I don't know why. Whenever she went into a new situation she fought like a cornered animal," the previous foster mother said. "She kept me constantly in sight, clinging to my legs, and wailing. Because of this behavior, we couldn't take her out with us. She can't stand birthday or Christmas parties. The noise and commotion overwhelm her."

After eighteen months, the law allows CPS to begin proceedings for terminating parental rights, thus freeing the child up for adoption. Although the baby's mother hadn't been heard from in over two years, the law required that CPS attempt to notify her before the case went to court. When CPS found her, she requested a visit and refused to give permission for terminating her rights. Even though she never showed up for the scheduled visit, the paperwork had been stopped. There was however, one positive thing that came out of the encounter. At two-and-a-half years old, Baby Girl finally had a name: LaKeisha.

"I had to force CPS into getting her name from the mom," the previous foster mother told me. "Schools require children to have names before they can enroll, so I couldn't put her into daycare without one. Can you imagine not naming a child for almost three years?"

"Children's Protective Services arranged to have
LaKeisha attend daycare with normal children her age. She was
already developmentally delayed and falling further behind
everyday -- she needed help. Like Sammy, LaKeisha could
have qualified for a special education preschool program with
highly trained teachers and low child to staff ratio, but
LaKeisha went to ordinary daycare because the foster mother
had requested it. All the special education classes had waiting
lists several months long.

LaKeisha was almost three years old, but could say no
more than five understandable words, and spent her days in
school cowering in a corner away from the other children.
When she got home, she clung to the foster mother, cried, and
never let her out of sight. After six months of this, the foster
mother asked to have her moved.

————————

When I first saw her, LaKeisha's thick black hair was
fixed in numerous ponytails held with small, multicolored
barrettes. She was cute in a funny sort of way, but her wide-set
eyes were glazed and dull. Not only was she stick thin, but she
had a sunken, retracted chest and a deep cough. Not looking
forward to caring for another sickly child, I took her to the
doctor hoping treatment would end the problem quickly, before
the rest of the family caught whatever she had. The doctor
diagnosed bronchitis and wrote a prescription for antibiotics.

I discussed my concerns about LaKeisha's health with
the caseworker. "I think something's wrong with her teeth. One
has already fallen out and another one is loose. She needs to
see a dentist. Her doctor is treating her for bronchitis but he
said an expert should evaluate her retracted chest to see if
exercises would help. She also needs a developmental
evaluation. Her previous foster mother told me she was
supposed to be evaluated for developmental delays, and is on a
waiting list."

"There isn't any money for new clients in Children's
Medical Hospital unless their condition is life threatening,"
LaKeisha's caseworker explained. "But you can take her to any
Medicaid doctor. Her previous caseworker was supposed to

have sent in a request for developmental testing six months ago. I'll try to find out if there's any paperwork on it. With over a hundred kids, our caseloads are so full it's hard to get everything done."

Soon after her arrival, LaKeisha celebrated her third birthday. She stared at the candles but had no idea what to do and smiled blankly while the kids encouraged her to blow them out. Alice and Ben blew the candles out for her. She ate the cake with her fingers.

"She doesn't even know how to use a spoon," Alice said. "I guess we have a lot to teach her."

"I'm sure glad to have you as my helper, Alice." I hugged my daughter.

LaKeisha lacked even the most basic care skill and it was clear she needed to be taught. Instead of feeding her, as she seemed to expect, I held the spoon in her hand and guided the food to her mouth until she learned to do it herself. Alice, who was nearly eight, pitched in and helped.

Teaching dressing wasn't difficult. We started with undressing and used the backward chaining approach, which had been so successful with Rosey. I took LaKeisha's T-shirt off as far as her ears and waited for her to remove it from the top of her head. At first, she sat stubbornly on her bed with the T-shirt covering her face.

Once she overcame her stubborn resistance about doing anything for herself, I was able to teach her the basic self-care skills that most three year olds know. Her difficulty in learning reflected the difference between a normal child, who absorbs things from their environment without apparent effort, and a developmentally delayed child who must be tediously taught even simple skills.

The caseworker was doing her best though, and after LaKeisha's third birthday she arranged to have her evaluated. LaKeisha tested low in every area. She was between eighteen months and two years in her mental development. Her height and weight were in the bottom fifth percentile for a three year old. She could hear normally but her language was only at a six month old level. Under the recommendation of the M-team, her name was added to the waiting list for a special education class.

LaKeisha's problems didn't stop with learning difficulties. She had physical problems, also. I took LaKeisha to the doctor but he found no signs of malnutrition. I didn't know such extreme skinniness was common among children with Fetal Alcohol Syndrome. She looked as though she had been half-starved to death.

LaKeisha caught bronchitis and upper respiratory infections and the doctor could do nothing more than keep her on antibiotics. I wanted a specialist to see her, but CPS said there wasn't any money.

In addition to health problems, LaKeisha was terrified of anything new. When she entered my home for the first time, she screamed at the sight of my small dog. She grabbed onto my leg and clung as if her life depended on it. Her scrawny body shivered with fear and her cry was high pitched and terror-filled. I locked the dog outside and introduced the two gradually. It took LaKeisha a few days to begin petting the gentle animal and soon they were friends.

Each new experience terrified her. I walked LaKeisha through he house and showed her each piece of furniture, the fish tank, and her toys. She tensed her body tightly, cried, shivered, struggled, and clung to me. Sitting at the dinner table brought struggles and tears. So did lying on the dressing table for a diaper change. One by one, LaKeisha slowly got over her fears in the house. After a while, I began introducing her to the outside world. We took each step slowly, one experience at a time.

On her first trip to the grocery store, LaKeisha screamed and struggled when I tried putting her in the cart. Other shoppers stared at me critically, probably thinking what a spoiled child I had. Although embarrassed, I did my best to ignore them -- LaKeisha needed my full attention. After comforting and firm insistence, she settled down and even took an interest in shopping. Before I knew it, she began "helping" by pulling everything she could reach off the shelf and putting it into the cart.

LaKeisha was terrified of large open spaces and it took some time before she would go outside without screaming. On her first trip to the park, she clung to me fearfully. The other children tried drawing her into their games, calling her until, one hesitant step after another, she joined them. The swing soon became her favorite playground activity and she squealed in delight as I pushed her higher and higher. Along with Ben and Alice, she watched the tiny minnows in a stream meandering through the park. She clapped her hands and laughed when tomboy Alice climbed a tree -- really a large fallen log. I had the distinct impression this was the first time LaKeisha had ever been to a park or playground.

At home, LaKeisha spent her time clinging to my legs and tripping me as I tried walking around the house. When I attempted holding her, she cried, screamed, turned her head to avoid eye contact, and stiffened her body. If she didn't scream or cling, she whined.

LaKeisha didn't talk much, but I couldn't understand even the few words she did say. She couldn't understand me either. When I told her to sit down at the table for dinner, I never knew what she would do. She might cry as though she had been scolded or just smile blankly. Day after day, I took her hand and led her through each activity. Even though the other children were there for her to imitate, LaKeisha didn't catch on.

"Let's get in the car, we're going to the zoo!" I told the kids one warm spring day. Alice and Ben ran to the car, looking forward to this special treat. When LaKeisha saw me pick up Sammy's car seat, she knew I was leaving the house. This was one connection she did make. She clung to my legs, her cry piercing and desperate.

"You're coming too, LaKeisha. Get in the car." She knew I was going somewhere but didn't understand my words and continued clinging. When she finally realized I was taking her along, she beamed with pleasure.

During my University days, I had seen American Sign Language for the deaf used successfully as a bridge to help language delayed children learn to talk. When it became clear that funding problems would delay speech therapy, which the

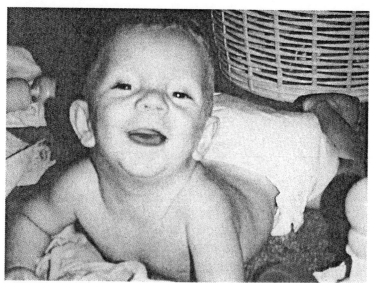

The baby pictured above has Fetal Alcohol Syndrome.

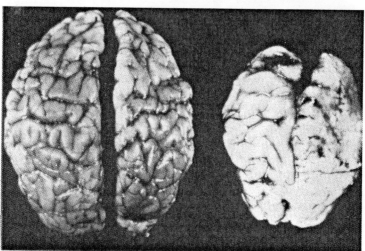

A normal brain (left) next to one from a person with Fetal Alcohol Syndrome. Photo courtesy of Anne Streissguth, University of Washington.

Linda Falkner

These photos are of a girl with Fetal Alcohol Syndrome at ages seven and twenty.

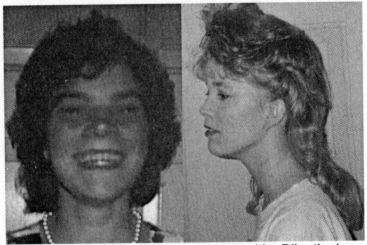

Left: Fetal Hydantoin Syndrome, caused by Dilantin, is easily mistaken for Fetal Alcohol Syndrome.

Right: Low, rotated ear is a common feature of Fetal Alcohol Syndrome.

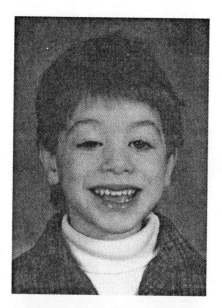

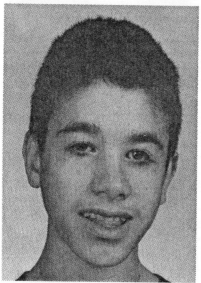

Boy with Fetal Alchol Syndrome and ptosis (droopy eye) at ages 5 (top) and 14.

multidisciplinary team had recommended, I decided to teach her myself. I'd seem disabled children learn a sign and soon after, begin saying the word. This is the same way a baby begins waving bye-bye just before learning to say the word. I am fairly fluent in sign language and decided to try a "sign bridge" with her.

"Here's an apple, LaKeisha," I said, holding an apple and signing. I bent her forefinger and moved it to her cheek to help her form the sign. I encouraged Ben and Alice to sign too. They enjoyed this new game. At first, LaKeisha watched passively but soon she began imitating signs. It wasn't long until she attempted words. "Ew" was easily understood when she also clapped her fisted hands together for the sign "shoe." This success encouraged her to continue talking and improving. The signs also seemed to help her sort out and understand my words. I kept my sentences short, only one idea at a time. Her memory was limited, but the signing helped her learn. In only a month, she learned twenty signs and spoke ten words clearly.

Toilet training was next. I tried the same technique I'd used with Rosey, but had no success. LaKeisha was terrified of both the adult toilet seat and the plastic baby potty. This was frustrating to both of us, and since it was going nowhere, I gave up for the time being. I later learned that children with Fetal Alcohol Syndrome are extremely difficult to toilet train, and it's not unusual for them to be only partially trained at seven and eight years old. I've even heard of FAS teenagers who still have toileting accidents, but at that age, it's more likely due to impulsiveness (I need to go right now and I don't want to stop what I'm doing to find a bathroom), or attention seeking, than lack of ability.

LaKeisha had more success in other areas, not all of which pleased me. As she became more independent, she learned to turn the doorknob and go outside into the fenced yard. I have never seen a child get dirty faster. I first learned that she could turn the doorknob when I was expecting company and had dressed her in her prettiest outfit. When my guests arrived, I took my eyes off LaKeisha only a second to open the door. In that short time she opened the back door and was gone. I found her a moment later coming in from the back yard covered with mud and a gritty face beaming with a pleased smile.

Then there were times when LaKeisha tried helping. She followed me around the house like a puppy and brought me gifts such as paper cups, napkins, small toys the kids had left on the floor, objects from the garbage, whatever else she could find. More than once, I almost tripped over her little body darting in front of me, smiling and holding up her newest offering. She was pleased with her "gift" and smiled with innocence.

As Sammy approached his first birthday and began playing with other children, he and LaKeisha became friends in the way of babies. She watched in fascination as he crawled about the floor and struggled to pull himself up and cruise along the furniture. She liked to "help" care for the baby and brought me a diaper whenever I put him on the dressing table. One afternoon she asked to feed him lunch. I was pleased to see LaKeisha want to do things not only for herself but for others, so I allowed her to try while I watched. Her motivation however, wasn't totally altruistic.

"H'r Ah-ee (here Sammy)," she said, placing a spoon in the babyfood jar and bringing it out, half empty and dribbling in the general direction of Sammy's mouth. The next spoonful went into her mouth. One for you and one for me -- sharing germs happens often when two young children live in the same household. One for you and two for me -- Sammy let out a protesting cry. "H'r," she said. The next spoonful almost went into Sammy's eye. I took over the feeding. LaKeisha would have to practice her spoon skills somewhere else.

Despite some cute times, I found myself grinding my teeth in frustration with LaKeisha. I felt exhausted and burned-out.

I called the social worker, "Can LaKeisha get into preschool for half-a-day until there's an opening in the special education class?"

"I thought you wanted to keep her home until she could get into that class."

"I did, but her constant clinging and whining is driving me nuts. I need to have a break sometimes."

A few days later the caseworker called. "I have the paperwork signed for LaKeisha's daycare. I labeled her as an "at risk" child. That puts her at the top of the line when Title XX (twenty) has an opening. They're usually filled up right after summer, but we can try."

"I thought Title XX was just for abused children living with their parents," I said. "Doesn't CPS pay for daycare?"

"No, we go through Title XX. They do more than just supervise preschool children who are at risk of abuse from their natural parents. It can also be a 'last ditch' effort to keep a difficult child from totally burning out the foster parents."

The Title XX office was in a rundown part of town, inside an ancient brick building that was originally built as a high school. The long empty hallway echoed from my footsteps as I walked through it.

In contrast to the hallway, the Title XX room was filled with people. I signed-in and waited on a small wooden folding chair. The walls were decorated with bright children's pictures. There was a small waiting area for children with crayons and toys on a small picnic table. The bulletin board was covered with pages of government laws in small, nearly illegible print. People were shifting in uncomfortable chairs, trying to keep their children quiet, waiting impatiently for the next available social worker.

When my turn came, the social worker gave me a list of Title XX schools and daycare centers, but warned me that most were closed. She gave me paperwork to take home and fill out. I needed to get LaKeisha's Social Security and Medicaid numbers.

I visited the schools on the list and discovered great differences in the quality of the various programs. One had over fifty babies, with row after row of cribs looking like so many prison cells. Children were taken out, changed, fed, and put back as part of an assembly line approach.

I tried putting the thought of this daycare out of my mind and quickly went on to the next.

The preschool I finally decided on was a well-run educational program just a few blocks from my home. I toured the school and the director told me they had openings in the two-year-old room. This is where they would put LaKeisha because although she was three, she wasn't toilet trained and didn't talk much. I agreed. The two-year-old class would challenge her.

I returned to the Title XX office and spoke with a caseworker. "I saw some of the schools on the list and have decided on this one. They told me they have an opening for LaKeisha."

"No, all the Title XX slots are filled for that school. They can take as many private pay children as they want, but we only place a specific number of Title XX children in each school. There is only one daycare with any slots left open. That 's the only program you can put her in."

When I visited, I understood why this was the last school to fill it's allotted slots. It was small, overcrowded, and in a rough area of town forty-five minutes from my house each way, an hour and a half round trip twice a day.

After visiting this school, I returned to the Title XX office for the third time in as many days.

"Do you want this space or not? If you don't, there's another child waiting for it, and we won't have any more openings until fall."

LaKeisha clung to my leg, pulled on my shirt and whined. "Okay," I said, remembering my promise to myself. Without a daily break, I couldn't keep her much longer. Although it was out of his way, Gary promised to help pick her up from the daycare on his way home from work.

LaKeisha showed no sign that she either liked or disliked daycare. She went willingly, if not happily.

"She spends all day sitting in the corner," her teacher told Gary. "Occasionally she
picks up a toy, but she never plays."

We heard daily complaints from the staff.

"You're late," the director met me at the locked gate one morning at ten minutes past eight. "If you can't get LaKeisha here by eight o'clock when I lock the gate, then don't bother bringing her at all that day. I'll let her stay today, but don't expect such special treatment again."

Mornings in our house were hectic. Gary got Sammy up and dressed first -- his bus come early. After Sammy was ready for school, I got Ben and Alice up and coaxed them to hurry as I dressed LaKeisha. After the last shoe was tied and bowl of cereal eaten, I put all three children in the car and dropped Alice and Ben off at their school, a few blocks from the house. The next hour and a half was spent driving through rush hour traffic to take LaKeisha to school and return home. Then I had a few hours to straighten up the house and do laundry before it was time for the kids to arrive home.

It was during these few childless hours that I began writing. I knew someday I would write about my children, but this wasn't the time. I wrote a story about a frazzled housewife who was repeatedly kidnapped by strong, handsome men who whisked her off to desert islands and other romantic places and made mad passionate love to her.

My home had become a nightmare and this fantasy world gave me the respite I needed to keep my sanity. Bedtime was always an ordeal. LaKeisha cried and repeatedly climbed out of bed. Unless someone stayed with her until she fell asleep, LaKeisha would get out of bed and break or destroy things. She pulled down curtains, broke window screens, and poured water onto the carpet. To keep LaKeisha in bed, someone had to sit with her for two or three hours. I had other children to get to bed, so I hired a teenaged neighbor to sit with her. Even then, I couldn't trust LaKeisha not to wake at three in the morning and wreak havoc. She loved pouring cups of water over furniture or electrical appliances in the middle of the night. Once she turned up the heater and we woke in the morning sweating. The house was over 90 degrees and the heater was running full blast.

In spite of the promise I made to myself to keep her, I felt as though I couldn't take many more and wanted LaKeisha moved. Looking back, I realize what an impossible promise this was, and how new I was to have believed I could keep it. I was fighting with myself about this, going back and forth in my mind. Moving a child should always be a last resort -- but what about Alice, Ben, and Sammy? They neither liked nor disliked LaKeisha, she was just there, but they needed my attention.

LaKeisha had to establish stability with one family, but how could I balance everyone's need? Maybe Ruth would have some suggestions, as she was good with difficult children. But when I called her, Ruth was having her own crisis. Pixie was missing. She had run away.

A judge devotes only five to ten
minutes when deciding a child's fate.

LAST BUT NOT LEAST

R uth was almost hysterical with worry but she was also angry. "Pixie threw rocks at the windows and broke them. Then she ran away. She's quite impressionable and will do whatever her friends tell her to do, without thinking about the consequences. Anything could happen. If she calls you, please let me know."

I promised I would. Ruth gave me some of Pixie's pills, strong medicine known as anti-psychotics, or major tranquilizers. "If she shows up, give these to her immediately. Don't let her in your house without them," she warned. "She had the potential to be dangerous when she's off her medicine."

Pixie called later and asked to visit. She took her medicine willingly and spent the day playing with LaKeisha and my other children. They were thrilled having Pixie there and so was I. She was pleasant and attentive -- the perfect playmate for the children and a mother's helper for me. Pixie had as much energy as three-year-old LaKeisha and kept her entertained while giving me some breathing space for a few hours. *Maybe the children's behavior isn't as bad as it seems,* I thought.

Pixie told me about the fight she'd had with Ruth and made it sound like a normal mother-teenager disagreement. However, she didn't mention the broken windows and I didn't bring the subject up either. When I took Pixie home later that evening, she seemed happy to go. Despite Ruth's trouble with her, she was always a delightful young lady at my house.

I decided to try harder with LaKeisha. After all, what was a little whining and clinging compared to a child who breaks windows and runs away? *I have it easy,* I told myself. But I wasn't convinced.

Living with LaKeisha was becoming more impossible every day. I could make it through each week, but began dreading the weekends when there was no school, and for me, no relief. The destruction to my house was increasing. LaKeisha seemed to have gotten over her earlier fear of water and now it fascinated her. She poured water on everything. Furniture was discolored, my clock radio never worked again after being soaked, and a new wooden floor was warped beyond repair. CPS told me to contact *my* insurance company because their insurance funds were used up for the next two years.

The car ride to school didn't always go smoothly, either. LaKeisha learned to unlock the car door and open it. I first learned that she could do this while driving on the expressway. Fortunately, I was near the exit and pulled over immediately. When I moved her car seat to the front where I could keep a closer watch one her, she grabbed the steering wheel and the car swerved into the next lane while I struggled to regain control. The car behind me blasted its horn long and hard. My wild driving had almost caused an accident.

One morning while the children were getting into the car, LaKeisha darted ahead and ran into the street. Our street was quiet and there was little traffic, but still, this was forbidden behavior, and LaKeisha knew it. I felt as though the situation with this child was becoming more and more unmanageable.

Distraught and unable to sleep, I stayed up long hours writing my fantasy story. My plain Jane housewife escaped across the vast ocean on a great white, winged horse. She found herself on a desert island with a muscular, handsome man who heroically saved her life throughout several adventures. Best of all, there were no children anywhere.

Back in the real world, the weekend was coming. Gary would take Alice, Ben, and Sammy out for the day but the weekend meant LaKeisha would spend Friday afternoon until Monday morning at home, I wouldn't have a moments rest. I felt suffocated by her constant demands.

I called the caseworker, asking if some form of respite were available, and in response she implied that I was neglecting LaKeisha. After all, why wasn't I awake and watching her at four in the morning and why was I spending time caring for my other three children? LaKeisha was in daycare four hours a day, wasn't this enough of a break for me? Besides, her behavior wasn't really so bad, nothing that constant attention twenty-four hours a day couldn't solve. The caseworker was new to her job, and thought I was exaggerating when I told her how frustrating caring for LaKeisha was. How much trouble could one tiny three year old *really* be?

"Don't worry about it, she won't be staying with you much longer anyway," she said. "I've contacted LaKeisha's birth mother and invited her to visit the child. She'll see LaKeisha next week. Is it all right if she visits at your house?"

"It's okay," I said reluctantly, not really wanting her in my home. "Although I doubt she'll show up."

"If she doesn't come, the courts will release LaKeisha for adoption. This is her mother's last chance."

As I anticipated, LaKeisha's birth mother never came for the visit. She had disappeared again and no one knew where to contact her.

Each day dragged on, becoming more difficult than the previous one. I had locks on my doors, locks on my gate, locks everywhere. I kept LaKeisha with me at all times. Wherever I went, she went. She became my constant companion, my shadow.

Ben often tried playing with LaKeisha. She watched but couldn't understand or join his games.

"She's not any fun Mom," he complained. "All she wants to do is hang onto your leg, and she's always crying."

Alice had her own idea about foster children. "I wish Pixie was my foster sister instead of LaKeisha. She's fun."

Before long, Gary refused to watch LaKeisha. "She only wants you," he said.

Adult babysitters wouldn't come anymore.

Even the daycare workers were reluctant to see her arrive. She spent her time in daycare sitting under a table crying. She refused to interact with the teachers, and screamed with fear when the other children approached her. Sometimes she threw toys, or pushed them off shelves, but never played with them.

I talked to the caseworker again. "LaKeisha has worn me out. Even with daycare and a teenaged babysitter helping out on school nights, I can't maintain a twenty-four hour a day vigilance. Between LaKeisha and my other kids, I'm exhausted.

"No problem, I can find another home easily," the neophyte caseworker said. "She's going to be freed for adoption soon and as cute as she is, I'm sure it won't be difficult finding her an adoptive home."

When foster children are moved repeatedly, it interferes with any attachment they may form with their foster families. Each move increases the chance that a child will not be able to bond again and this accelerates that downward spiral leading to emotional, learning, and behavioral problems. When this happens, the child becomes more and more unruly, and therefore loses the next placement even sooner. I hated moving LaKeisha, but she was already on this spiral, and I was no longer able to give Alice, Ben, or Sammy the time and attention they needed because she was draining everything from me.

Three weeks after LaKeisha left, I received a phone call. "Hello, I'm LaKeisha's new foster mother. I found your phone number in her file. What can you tell me about her? I've had her four days and I doubt I can last the week."

We talked for a few minutes and I wished her luck.

LaKeisha had spent six months in the foster home before mine, one month with me, two weeks in the next home and now, four days later, she was about to lose another placement.

I had gone into foster care with the intension of helping children, but now I realized I'd entered a flawed system and had become part of it. If I wanted to raise my own two children in a healthy environment, then keeping every child placed with me was an impossible goal. Yet, every time I asked to have a child moved, knowing what I was doing tore me up inside. I decided that Sammy would be my last foster child, although I would keep him as long as possible. Gary and I even talked about adopting him if his mother ever signed release papers.

When Sammy first started the half-day special school program, he cried or withdrew into sleep. This is common among substance-exposed babies and the school was prepared to handle such problems. He was transferred from the regular baby room into the infant quiet-room with its carpeted floor and sound absorbing walls. There, he began waking up and taking an interest in his surroundings. He did so well that he soon became a favorite with the staff.

He continued improving at home also. By ten months he was responding consistently to sounds and responded to his name. He looked at the correct person when asked, "Where's Mommy, Daddy, Alice, Ben, or Pixie?"

Pixie regularly visited "her baby" after school, and spent many afternoons rocking and playing with him. He had become her love. There were times however when I didn't hear from Pixie for weeks. She was my main contact with Ruth, as we were both too busy with disturbed children to have much time for a social life. I talked to Ruth on the phone occasionally, such as when Pixie turned eighteen.

"Pixie's out of my house and I'm not letting her back in. She's in the mental hospital because she threw a hot frying pan at me. The police took her away in handcuffs -- she was like a wild animal. I have two new foster children so there's no room in my house for her now," Ruth said. Did I tell you that CPS took the last child out of my home without any notice at all? The caseworker just drove up my house and took him. She didn't even call ahead. He was returned to his mother but I doubt it will last long."

"I guess I'm lucky," I said. "They usually give me at least a few weeks notice."

"It's different with each caseworker." Ruth fell silent. I could see how distressed she was and I shared her concern for the child's welfare. I knew the same thing could happen to my foster children and prayed it never would.

"Joseph got a new job in another state. We're quitting foster care and moving at the end of the month." Ruth changed the topic.

When Ruth and Joseph moved, Pixie was left on her own. She was eighteen, had not yet finished high school, and had the maturity of a ten year old, at best. She had been a ward of the state all her life and now her caseworker said, "You're an adult. Go out and take care of yourself."

Shortly after Sammy was born, his mother disappeared. She left without informing Children's Protective Services of her whereabouts. Sammy's caseworker didn't know that his mother was in a drug rehabilitation program until she was released and called to see her baby.

"Sammy will begin having hourly visitations with his mother at the CPS office twice a month," the caseworker informed me. The next week a driver picked him up for his first visit but brought him home sooner than I had expected.

"What happened?" I asked.

"His mother never showed up." She handed the baby to me.

I was glad. I loved Sammy, and so did Gary and the kids. I'd raised this baby from birth and nursed him through the suffering his mother's alcohol and drug addiction had caused. I knew she had also been a foster child and was as much a victim of the system as he was, but I didn't feel sympathetic towards her. We were all hoping Sammy would be freed for adoption.

Later that week I met the caseworker at the CPS building. I can no longer remember the reason why I was there, however, I do remember a woman walked past us, briefly glanced into the stroller at Sammy, and then walked on.

"Shh," the caseworker said. "That's Sammy's mother. She didn't recognize him."

The second visit was during Sammy's naptime and when she returned him still sleeping, the caseworker reported, "His mother held and rocked him while he slept. You wouldn't believe how happy she was to see him. She just rocked him and cried. I think they've adequately bonded and we can begin plans for returning him home. She's managing to stay off drugs and has a job and an address now. Is it okay for her to call you? You can't call her because she doesn't have a phone."

"Of course, my number's listed in the book. She can call and check on her son anytime she wants."

Many foster parents don't allow their numbers to be given to parents, but I did. If Sammy was to return to his birth mother, there was nothing I could do to stop it. The more she knew about him, the easier the transition would be, and the better for the baby. However, it didn't surprise me when she never called -- he wasn't a baby she knew, or had anything invested in. She hadn't cared for herself during her pregnancy, and the forced separation had broken any bond between them before it had a chance to develop. But even though they were strangers, he was still her baby, and like any mother, it broke her heart to have him taken away. Sammy's mother wanted him back, and CPS wanted to return him, but I questioned his mother's commitment and ability to care for him.

Shortly before Sammy's return home, there was a court hearing and the caseworker invited me to come and meet the mother. She was a thin, nervous woman whose normal features contrasted sharply with her son's oddly shaped Fetal Alcohol Syndrome features. She looked at me suspiciously. I felt like cringing under her icy stare but instead, hoping she would be interested in knowing about her son, I talked about the progress he was making. I told her that he could cruise along furniture and I was sure he would be walking soon. She didn't answer with words but began sobbing. To have her baby taken away, against her will, must have been unbearably painful. Other women with children in foster care have told me that the loss of a child is always heartbreaking. I can't imagine that it could have been any other way for Sammy's birthmother.

The caseworker fidgeted in her chair. The situation was awkward and uncomfortable for everyone. I waited outside the room while Sammy's mother and the caseworker talked to the judge. It took just a few minutes. The caseworker later told me that Sammy's mother only needed to complete a parenting skills class, which CPS taught, and take a drug test before they would return him.

After the court date, Sammy's mother continued having supervised visits with him in the CPS office for an hour every other week. She continued missing visits though, and had no other contact. She never called to inquire about him.

As the time for his return grew near, I began reminding myself that Sammy was not really my child and would be leaving soon. But no preparation is ever enough to steel me against the depression, which closes over my life whenever a child I love, leaves my home.

Ben and Alice were upset too. Sammy had been with us for nearly a year. He was part of our family now, and I knew we would all feel a loss when he left. I continued reminding them that he'd be going back to his "real" mother soon. I wanted to make the transition as easy as possible for everyone. The kids were sad, but they understood.

Sammy however, was far too young to understand this change, which would affect him the most of all. I talked to his caseworker several times, and she arranged to have Sammy continue in the same school. The less disruption in his life, the better.

Unexpectedly, the caseworker called me one evening. "Sammy will be leaving your house tomorrow morning. His mother has completed her performance plan so we need to return him to her. The judge thinks she's ready to take him now."

"Tomorrow?" All the knowledge that he would be going and all the planning hadn't prepared me for such a sudden departure. I wasn't ready. I'd cared for this baby for eleven months. Now, suddenly, overnight, I would no longer have the right to see him or even know anything about him. Legally, he belonged to a stranger.

I reflected over the past year. I had put up with false abuse allegations, trying to raise children with inadequate financial reimbursement, no respite, little support or respect, but the final loss of this child, a decision made by a judge who had never met either Sammy or me, was the final insult. One third of children return to foster care after being returned to their birth parents, and when children like Sammy are returned to unprepared birth parents, they may be in danger of being neglected, abused, or even worse. Some have been killed. I couldn't continue being a part of this system any longer.

I packed his clothes, asthma medicine, and antibiotics. I wrote a long note to his mother, telling her everything I could think that she needed to know about him. Sammy crawled around the floor, pulled himself up on the furniture and walked holding on with both hands. He smiled an odd crooked smile, looked me in the eyes and babbled. He had come so far this year. Oh, I would miss him, and so would the children. Sammy was my last foster *baby* and my last *official* foster child.

The summer was wonderful. It had been so long since I'd had only Ben and Alice -- now they were no longer babies. Without any infants to take along, we were free to go to the beach or park on a whim. They kids loved our new found freedom.

Ruth and Joseph moved and we lost touch, but Pixie stayed in town. She called me occasionally to pick her up, and every time she was living in a different place -- a boarding home, a group home for senior citizens, a family who let her stay with them temporarily, or a mental hospital. None of these places seemed quite right for her, and she never called from the same place twice. She was quite a nomad. That summer she often joined us on our outings and the kids always looked forward to having their "big sister" along. Once I took the kids for ice cream and the waitress mistook Pixie for one of my children, referring to her as my daughter. Pixie and I laughed about this. I realized then that she had truly become part of us.

"Do you think I'm pretty?" Pixie asked one day.

I couldn't answer her. Her long black braids swing freely. Her eyes shine. Her smile reaches across her face when she laughs, a smile that makes her friends wherever she goes. Some people find her wide set eyes striking, and some find her beautiful. But when I look at her, I see the damage drugs and alcohol have done, and I know the life she should have had is permanently lost.

*People who work with those affected
by Fetal Alcohol Syndrome learn to
appreciate their childlike innocence.*

THE FOREVER CHILD

T he summer heat abated and the first hint of fall
followed. There was sharpness in the early morning air
and the trees began weaving red, orange and brown
into their green. School started and the children, full with
excitement and anticipation, went off to their new grades toting
brand new backpacks, pencils, and a variety of miscellaneous
must haves.

The days were shortening and it was already dusk
when Pixie called. I hadn't heard from her in a while, but I was
used to her popping in and out of my life at the most
unexpected times. I had no way of knowing tonight would be
any different.

"Linda, I'm really sick and need you to take me to the
emergency room. Can you please come?"

I looked at my watch. It was a school night so Ben and
Alice needed to go to bed early. "What's the matter?" I asked.

"I can't eat, or keep anything down. I'm dehydrated. I
called the hospital and they want to see me right away."

"Can't the staff at your boarding home take you?" I
asked. I was sure someone at her supervised facility would
make sure she got adequate medical care.

"No, it's against their policy, but I'm really sick."

Her voice sounded weak, and she convinced me she needed immediate medical attention. "I can drop you off and pick you up later. I've got to get my kids to bed and can't wait there with you. Where are you living now?"

Pixie moved so often I never knew where she lived. Over the past year she had kept contact intermittently. In spite of this, the kids and I had grown close to her. Often I'd wonder about her, and then she'd call that same day. It was as though there was spiritual communication between us. She gave me the address and directions to her newest home.

I arrived at Garden House, a supervised adult boarding home for residents with mental, emotional, and physical disabilities that limited their ability to live alone. The facility resembled a two-story motel with a dozen separate doors exiting from a single building. A long driveway and thick bushes hid it from the road and provided privacy. The door to Pixie's "apartment" opened into an empty living room connected the two bedrooms. There were two girls per bedroom. Each resident had a twin bed and a dresser. There was no other furniture in the room. Meals were prepared by the staff and served in a community room.

Pixie was waiting for me when I arrived, standing with a grungy young man. He was drooling and he let the drool hang from his lip, seemingly unaware of it. His hands shook, his clothes were old, stained, and torn, and his hair dirty and unbrushed.

Pixie introduced us. "This is my boyfriend, Richard. Is it okay if he comes along to keep me company?"

Pixie had often talked about her boyfriend but I'd never met him. I was surprised that this perky young girl would feel attracted to such a raggedy and dirty person.

"Okay," I said. "I'll take you to Doctor's Hospital."

"No, I need to go to Medical."

"It's only a few blocks to Doctors. Medical is halfway across town."

"But Medical has my records. My ulcer is acting up again."

I hadn't planned on the longer drive, but Pixie looked pale and was insistent that she needed the further hospital. It almost made sense -- at the time.

Just as we arrived at the hospital, Pixie began making vomiting sounds. An aide brought a wheelchair and rushed her into the emergency room.

Several hours later Gary picked to kids up, took Richard home, and brought Pixie to our house. She'd been given and I.V. for dehydration.

"Didn't the doctor give you medicine for your throwing up?" I asked.

"No," Pixie shrugged her shoulders.

"I'm going to the store to get you something that might help."

"I'll come along." She doubled over with stomach pains and could barely walk.

"You don't look good. Stay here and rest."

"No, I'm okay. I really want to come along," she insisted in a child's voice. "I'll stay in the car."

The motion sickness pills seemed to help. She had stopped taking her medication for seizures and emotional problems, but now that the vomiting was under control, she told me she was again taking her medicine.

Pixie was too ill to return to the boarding home so I invited her to stay the night and she readily agreed. She recovered slowly and three days later was still with us. I took her to the boarding home to get clothes. She went into her room while I informed the staff that she'd be spending a few more days with me. When I returned to Pixie's room I found her sitting on the bed crying.

"I've been robbed," she said. "The door was forced open and someone's gone through my drawers. I'm missing all my money and Richard's radio. He loaned it to me. Someone rode my bike and bent the wheel. I can't live in this terrible place anymore."

Back at my house, Pixie filed a police report and her adult level of competency while she talked to the officers impressed me. Pixie was not always so mature. Often she became fearful or stressed and regressed to a younger age.

"Sometimes I act babyish," she said. "When that happens, tell me to grow up. It's just a bad habit."

Pixie didn't want to return to the boarding home. She still felt ill and I spent everyday that week taking her to various doctor appointments while my kids were in school. Her doctors were concerned enough to consider exploratory surgery to find the cause of her chronic stomachaches and nausea. The operation was tentatively scheduled in two weeks so Pixie would have time to recover her strength.

Pixie's diet was limited to bland baby food, applesauce, and toast. She could never have eaten the greasy food served at the boarding home. Pixie was a picky eater anyway, and I often had to remind her to eat.

Alice and Ben tasted the baby food and hated it. "How can you eat that? Do you really like it?" they asked Pixie. She thrived on the attention.

Although she still wasn't feeling well, she was so cheerful and fun that I loved having her around. She told stories to my children, sang and played with them, bathed and brushed our dog, and even mowed the yard once. Her high mood was contagious and we were all having a good time. Pixie filled the empty space our last foster child, Sammy, had left. Gary and I had a family discussion with Alice and Ben about Pixie. We unanimously agreed to invite her to move in with us permanently. That was when she began calling me "Mom," and Gary "Dad." She'd already been referring to Alice and Ben as her sister and brother.

Alice was especially excited over Pixie staying. Here was her "dream come true," older sister. But I knew from Pixie's history, and warned Alice, that Pixie was likely to move out as suddenly as she had moved in.

I didn't tell my excited children how nervous Pixie's past made me feel. There were a lot of unknowns about her. I knew that children who have grown up in foster care have trouble getting close to, or bonding with other people, and they often don't have much conscience. This is even truer when the children are prenatally substance-exposed like Pixie. Ruth confirmed Pixie's story about her mother being an alcoholic, and Pixie's facial features suggest that she has Fetal Alcohol

Syndrome (FAS). I expected problems, but I had known her for two years and in the last few days she had brought fun and joy back into our home. Whatever came up, we could overcome. We just needed time -- and patience.

Pixie moved everything she owned into our house. There was a broken bike small enough for an eight year old, a plastic garbage bag half filled with clothes, a small box containing fish hooks, a hairbrush and toothbrush labeled with her name. She had another plastic garbage bag full of papers and balls of yarn, and to my surprise, a bag of adult sized diapers. This was everything Pixie had collected in her nineteen years of life.

Pixie attended a daycare program for homeless mentally ill people. She had services such as case-management, psychiatric medical care, social activities, and respite (the adult equivalent of having a babysitter). Her case-manager, Mary, didn't know me and was concerned about her moving in with my family.

"You don't have many friends and I don't want you burning anymore bridges," Mary said to Pixie. "I'm going to keep you on the waiting list for the half-way house, just in case it doesn't work."

Mary suggested that Pixie attend the Graduate Equivalence Degree program, which would prepare her for the high school equivalence test (GED). Pixie wanted to enroll in high school, but after some pouting she acquiesced and entered the GED program for one day. That evening, while her boyfriend Richard was visiting, she began complaining about her GED class.

"Mom, this work is too hard."

"Let me see," I said. "This isn't hard. I'll bet you can get this first problem. What is three plus zero?"

Pixie mumbled to herself and attempted counting on her fingers. I might just as well have asked her to explain Einstein's Theory of Relativity. Not only was Pixie unable to understand math but she also couldn't read the simplest children's stories. Her printing showed numerous backward letters, although she could write perfectly in cursive.

Alice and Ben were incredulous. "I can do that," said five-year-old Ben, showing off his reading and counting skills.

Pixie said nothing.

It was hard to believe she had such severe problems and still made it most of the way through high school. She must have been in a certificate program. I knew mentally disabled children were given certificates of attendance after twelve years in school. The though occurred to me that she might be faking, but why would anyone act so impaired on purpose, especially in front of a new family and boyfriend? I remembered Ruth talking about Pixie's learning disabilities, but she'd never indicated anything this severe. Now, I wondered how much Pixie was able to learn.

The evening was getting late and I suggested it was time for Richard to go home. The kids excused themselves to take showers and get ready for bed. Pixie, who never washed without being reminded, went to bathe while I tried getting Richard to leave.

"It's really to late to take the bus. Do you think you can drive me home?" he asked.

"I'm sorry, Rick, but it's the kid's bedtime. You agreed to take the bus home tonight." I knew this wasn't really a problem for him.

"Well, the bus may have stopped running for the night. I'll have to walk, I guess."

Just then, Pixie came out of the bathroom wrapped in a towel. While she might have been mentally a child that night, she certainly was not one physically.

"You need to go now," she said.

"How about a good-bye kiss?" Richard said, looking at her towel covered body with bugged eyes.

"No. Goodbye."

Richard left -- for awhile."

Soon the phone rang. Richard was at the corner drug store suffering from chest pains. Gary took Pixie and Richard to the hospital, but Richard's pains stopped and the doctors could find nothing physically wrong. From his disappearing symptoms, and poor hygiene, the doctors suggested the pain was psychosomatic in nature.

When Pixie first arrived, her hair was stringy and unwashed, and her bangs hung over her eyes. The grown out layer cut accentuated her disheveled appearance. Now that she decided to stay, it was time to cut her hair. I began trimming her bangs, and in my enthusiasm, cut them too short. Her appearance startled me and I stepped back a moment.

"What's wrong Mom?" she asked.

"Sorry, I slipped and cut your bangs too short. They'll grow out soon enough." I had been startled, not by the poor haircut, but the small size and odd shape of her forehead, hidden beneath the bangs. I'd suspected from her behavior that Pixie had brain damage, but now I had no doubt. She couldn't possibly have a normal brain under that small, misshapen head.

My friend, Dianne, came over later and reminded me of the first haircut I'd ever given a foster child. "Do you remember when you messed up Valentine's first haircut? Pixie had that same tiny forehead. You'd better leave the haircuts to the pro's from now on."

"I'd forgotten about that," I laughed.

I took out my photo album and looked at the girl's pictures next to each other.

"The resemblance is striking. These pictures could be the same person at two different ages," Dianne said.

Soon Pixie began feeling better and like LaKeisha, she followed me everywhere I went. The only time she wasn't with me was the three times a week when her respite worker took her on an outing.

Pixie played with Alice and Ben as though she were a young child. My kids enjoyed her attention. Other than Richard, she didn't seem to have any friends her own age, and her relationship with him was confusing.

"Richard and I are going to get an apartment together," Pixie announced one day. "We're getting married."

"Have you thought about birth control?" I asked.

"I won't need any. We'll have twin beds. He's not really my boyfriend anyway. In fact, I don't even like him."

Pixie's surgery was just a few days away, but she was feeling better and expressing an interest in attending high school. She'd had difficulty in school and had dropped out after leaving Ruth's house on her eighteenth birthday. She had two years left to graduate.

"Do you have any clothes you can wear to school?" I asked.

"Just what I have here."

She had been wearing a short midriff T-shirt with the word CRABBY printed across the front and shorts with a mismatched checkered pattern. Her other clothes were equally inappropriate for school.

I dropped Pixie off at the clothes store while I went shopping. Pixie chose one dress. When we got home she showed it to me. It was at least two sizes too big, but Pixie didn't seem to notice. I told her it would have to go back. I stayed close to Pixie on future shopping trips and checked the clothes before she bought them. She acted babyish in the store, used a high pitched, lisping speech, chewed on her watchband, and gave the general appearance of a three year old. She lacked judgment and picked out dresses that were either too loose, or so tight she could barely move.

Pixie had a Barbie doll figure. Tight midriffs showing her stomach and shorts would have looked great at the beach, or cute on a three year old, but not in a high school wardrobe.

Pixie would never stay home by herself, shadowed me constantly and required nonstop one-on-one attention, which I willingly gave her. She was cheery and I enjoyed her company.

After Alice and Ben came home from school, she played with them while I caught up on housework and prepared dinner. Pixie was fun. The kids enjoyed her "up" mood as much as I did. They loved having an almost grown-up join their games and they whispered silly jokes to each other, laughing hilariously.

In the evening, after the kids were asleep, Pixie told me stories about her life in foster care and institutions. The general theme was what a bad child she'd been and the trouble she'd gotten into. She also talked about her problems.

"I'm very sick," she said in her most adult voice. "I've been in eleven mental hospitals this year alone."

Eleven. One a month. How can that be?

"Why? What do you do?"

"I don't know. I just wake up and find myself in the hospital. I can't remember what happened. When I start acting babyish, people call the police and have me involuntarily put in the hospital. I have to stay at least three days for observation. The police come and put me in their car. I get scared and fight them. One time a policeman 'hog tied' me and locked handcuffs on my wrists and ankles. They were too tight. See the scar?" She held up her arm to show me her wrist, and then pulled it away before I could see if there really was any scar. "The policeman told me 'Meet Mr. Handcuff. I know all the police in town. I know all their handcuffs too!" She laughed. "Meet Mr. Handcuff!"

"What should I do if this happens?"

"Just put me in my room. If you leave me alone and give me time, I'll come out of it myself." Pixie looked down at the floor.

I knew she'd been hospitalized numerous time, but I also knew she sometimes entered the hospitals voluntarily. I wondered why she spent so much time in psychiatric hospitals.

"I need to warn you, when I get mad I pound my head and people say I throw things, although I can't remember."

"Doesn't pounding your head hurt?" I feigned surprise. Ruth had already told me about this but I found it hard to believe and wondered if she hadn't exaggerated the story. I had no clue how seriously ill Pixie was.

"No, I can't feel anything at all. I think it's some kind of seizure. I get another kind of seizure where my hand shakes and I can't stop it."

We talked late into the night. I promised not to commit Pixie to a hospital unless there was no other choice. I later realized this promise, like the one I had made to keep every foster child, was neither possible nor desirable.

Under my nurturing care, Pixie started feeling better and soon her boundless energy returned. She decided to take swimming lessons, then changed her mind and wanted ballet, then karate.

"Karate?" I asked. I hadn't forgotten her violent history.

"I love it and I've taken it before. I'll tell you what color belt I have," she said, paging through a book showing what colors can be earned. "I have a red belt! Like this one here," she lied. I knew she had picked red because it was her favorite color.

She'll probably take one class and lose interest. I'll let her go.

She began taking Karate twice a week and her respite worker continued picking her up for activities the other three days. But this wasn't enough activity for Pixie. Less than a week away from major surgery, she was anxious to start school. Pixie had already passed her eighteenth birthday, and although by law she qualified for emotionally handicapped classes in public school until she turned twenty-one, not many students entered school at this age. I talked to Mr. Everglow, the supervisor of the emotionally handicapped (E.H.) program and he agreed to contact her previous high school for her records. She could register as soon as the records arrived.

Pixie was impatient with the delay and pestered me to find another program. We both needed her to have more outside activities, so I spent several hours on the phone searching for alternative high school programs for adults. I found two. One was an adult day literacy program and the other was taught in the evening. The night class sounded perfect. It was individualized with computers. The instructor had a dual major in learning disabilities and emotional handicaps.

"I want to register tonight, Mom."

"You'll be late tonight. It's dark and I'm not sure where the school is. Lets wait for tomorrow. I need to finish cooking dinner and put the kids to bed."

"Please. I really need this. Please. I know where the school is and it's not far." She smiled and pleaded and begged nonstop until I finally agreed to take her. Gary was working late, so Alice and Ben came along. The three children sang, laughed and played guessing games in the old station wagon. Pixie had no idea where the school was located, and with only an unfamiliar street name, I didn't have a clue. Pixie seemed unconcerned and the subject of the night school never came up again. She had just wanted to go for a ride. All three kids had enjoyed the outing, but it was late and the kids were tired getting up for school the next morning. I'd put Pixie's wishes above the needs of my own children, and now I was angry with her, and with myself for giving in.

The next morning Pixie cheerfully helped get Alice and Ben ready for school as she usually did. I appreciated having the extra help every morning and forgave her manipulation from the night before. I resolved to be firmer in the future.

After the kids were in school, I took Pixie to the Adult Literacy program and helped her enroll. The top of the form asked for her name. She hesitated and carefully looked down the page as though searching for something.

"I can't find a P," she whispered. "How do you make one?"

I showed her with my finger and she wrote it -- backwards! Oh, she seemed so sincere and her eyes lit up with glee when she finally got the letter right. I completed the form and Pixie joined the class.

The children are all in school now, I thought. *I'll be glad to have my days back to myself.*

But I was wrong. Pixie brought home pages of papers with most of the letters reversed. It seemed clear that this class wasn't meeting her needs, either.

"I have a dentist appointment tomorrow so I can't go to school. I need you to drive me there," she said.

"What about your class?"

"I don't want to go anymore. I want to be in high school. Can you take me to the dentist tomorrow?" She gave me a heart-warming smile that I had trouble turning down. I later came to recognize this cuteness as one of her best tools of manipulation.

After taking her to the dentist, I called the high school and spoke with Mr. Everglow.

"Please bring Pixie in tomorrow and I'll help her register, he said. "By the way, I have her records. She reads at a sixth grade level and can do math at third grade. Her I.Q.

scores are in the low normal range. She's able to do a lot more than she's been letting on."

"I have no doubt." I hung up the phone. Pixie was listening to my conversation.

"Okay Pixie, time to fess up. How do you explain these scores?"

"I cheated. I copied from the other students." She looked directly in my eyes.

"No you didn't. Those were individualized tests. There were no other students."

"It must be the seizures. They were really bad and I've forgotten a lot."

How can she look so sincere and tell such an obvious lie?

The next morning, Pixie showered and brushed her hair without being reminded even once. She wore a pastel, flowered dress that complimented her slender teenaged figure.

When she arrived at the school, I noticed how young Pixie appeared compared to the other high school students. Her actions were babyish and she still reversed letters in her name.

Mr. Everglow came into the room and reprimanded her. "These are for your permanent records."

Pixie filled in the forms again, this time without the reversals. But she still wasn't ready to give up the game.

"Is this right?" she asked me as she printed each letter with great effort. She printed her name, dated, and signed the form, then gave it to me to finish.

"Come into my office and we can plan your schedule," Mr. Everglow said.

We followed him and Pixie shuffled her feet and chewed on her watchband. She looked and sounded very much like a two year old.

"Stop chewing on that," Mr. Everglow said sternly.

Pixie straightened up and looked more mature.

"I have to get some papers. I'll be back in a minute."

Pixie slouched and chewed her watchband until Mr. Everglow returned. I watched, learning her tricks.

"I want to take drivers education so I can get my license," Pixie said in an infantile, lisping voice.

Mr. Everglow decided she would take the usual high school class's part time, along with her emotionally disturbed classes.

"The drivers education class is already filled," he said tactfully.

Looking back, it was now becoming clear to me how much lying and manipulating Pixie had been doing over the past week. I was relieved she didn't have dyslexia on top of her other problems, but I was angry. I had spent all week running around, trying to get help for her non-existent problem.

Has she been laughing at me all this time, or has she just acted out to get my attention without thinking about the consequences? My mind was spinning with questions. *Does she have any conscience at all? Is it time to kick her out?*

I spoke with Gary, Alice, and Ben. The kids were still enjoying her company. They found her outrageous, but great fun. Besides having an additional adult in the house giving them attention, Pixie was always planning something special for them to do. Gary was neutral and said he would support whatever decision I made.

After some serious thought, I decided to let Pixie stay. I'd expected problems from the start and I enjoy a challenge. Not only did she have Fetal Alcohol Syndrome, but she had also grown up in foster care. She expected to be kicked out and was testing me. According to her, she had lived in more than a hundred homes with placements lasting from one week to three months. Knowing about the foster care system, I knew she could be telling the truth. Being kicked out was Pixie's expectation, but I wanted to be different. However, we needed a serious discussion and some changes if she was to stay much longer.

I looked around my old fashioned, wood framed house with its large windows on each wall. Pixie had lived in her last foster home with Joseph and Ruth for two years before breaking their windows. How would she react to a direct confrontation? I couldn't take a chance of violence in my home so I took her to a quiet restaurant where I thought she'd be less likely to act out. A neighbor watched Ben and Alice while I picked Pixie up from her Karate class. The restaurant was almost empty and the waitress seated us at a private table in the corner.

"I've brought you here to have a talk. We will have dinner at home." I was not about to reward her with a restaurant meal. "Do you know what I want to talk about?"

Pixie shrugged her shoulders but didn't answer.

"Take a guess," I said.

"My coming out of the bath with only a towel on in front of Richard?"

In the confusion of Richard's sudden illness and all the other chaos, I'd never gotten around discussing this with her. It must have been hanging over her head.

"That was wrong, and I'm glad you know it. What should you have done?"

Pixie shrugged her shoulders again and looked past me, "I should have waited for him to leave. But Alice came out in a towel, too."

"Alice is only a little girl. You're a young lady," I reminded her. Modesty was not a strong point for Pixie and I suspected this would continue being a problem.

"Now the other thing I wanted to talk about tonight is honesty. Do you know what that means?"

Pixie shrugged her shoulders and looked around as though she wanted to escape, but she was captive in the restaurant and had to listen to my requirements. Her continued placement in my home depended upon her agreement. When we arrived home, Pixie had a homework assignment. I wrote out a list of house rules and she copied them to hang next to her bed. One of the house rules was *I will be honest.* Another was *I will always do my best.*

"What do you think the consequences should be for breaking the house rules?" I asked Pixie.

"I could lose phone privileges for twenty-four hours. That would be fair."

"I think so, too."

The next week in our house was "honesty week." We read about honest people and talked about honesty. I did my best to demonstrate honest behavior. Alice and Ben are usually honest, although like all young children they occasionally tell a "fib," and the lesson was good for them. Pixie learned a new word, but her lying, manipulating, and rule breaking continued. She remained defiant and couldn't understand why she had to follow rules.

Friday night is children's services at our Temple and my kids enjoyed going. Pixie preferred to come rather than stay home alone. Instead of a sermon, our Rabbi dresses up in costume and acts out a story. He started by asking the children to "Tell me a rule your parents have that you don't like."

Pixie raised her hang along with the other children and the Rabbi called on her.

"We're not allowed to eat in the living room," she said.

"Oh, that's terrible!" the Rabbi exclaimed. He looked at me and winked, seeing this time the new child wasn't a baby.

The Rabbi's story was about a town where there were no rules. Mother's stole their children's ice cream cones. People had car accidents because they stopped at green lights and drove through red lights. Baseball games had a hundred or more people all playing at the same time and inventing their own rules as they played. The whole town was in chaos. In the end, the town decided to have rules and everyone was happy.

It was a tale I would remember and tell my children again.

"Thank you," I told the Rabbi. "That was a wonderful story."

*Alcohol is a major cause of birth defects and
mental retardation in this country, and the world.
It's also a drug with it's own lobby in Congress.*

BETWIXT

P ixie's eyes are small and this causes them to appear wide apart. There is a small fold of skin covering the inner corner, which leads some people to think she had Asian ancestry. She often gets compliments from strangers about her beautiful and unusual eyes. Her expressions are vibrant and her eyes glow with pleasure or anger. My friend, Dianne, who was now working as a psychiatric nurse, warned me she had seen such eyes in mental patients.

"How many people in mental hospitals do you suppose are affected by Fetal Alcohol Syndrome?"

"No, it's not the shape," she said, "It's the expression. She has the glazed look of someone who is schizophrenic. I think she's hallucinating. Are you checking to be sure she's taking her medicine?"

"She told me she is, but I'll check."

Later that evening when we were alone, I asked her about her medications.

She shrugged her shoulders.

"Could you show me what you take, please?"

"This is for seizures, this is for my hyperactivity, and I don't need this one anymore. I had a bladder infection but it's better now. That's why I had diapers."

"What is this?" I asked, finding an unopened box of prescription suppositories meant to stop vomiting.

"Oh, I don't like those. I never used them."

"Do you know why the doctor gave them to you?"

Another shoulder shrug.

"Here is a weekly pill box. Please put your pills in it to help you remember to take your medicine."

Pixie carefully organized her medication in the box. Every day she was supposed to take eighteen pills which were prescribed for seizures, mood-swings, depression, and psychosis. This was strong medicine with side affects that Pixie disliked. I was caring for an adolescent with more problems than I could ever have imagined two weeks ago. I had learned a lot since she came, but this was only the beginning.

The week before her exploratory surgery, Pixie started school.

"I love it!" She bounced into my car after her first school day. She chattered as I drove her to the doctor's office for a pre-surgery checkup.

"Only one problem, my biology teacher is a yuck. I don't't' need to take E.H. classes," she complained, "and I'm not going to take karate at the community center anymore. A private studio has given me a grant. I'll be able to go everyday, but I need a karate suit. Today."

"You'll get your allowance on Friday. I've already bought you school clothes and that's all I can afford."

Pixie had no sense of money -- especially mine. She fussed, fumed, yelled, and pleaded until allowance day arrived. Then she hurried to go shopping for the karate suit.

"Mom, look what I got," she showed me a small package.

"Where is the karate suit?"

"I need this more. Look, it's a diabetic bracelet and these are to stick my finger. I've been pre-diabetic since I was a young child. My doctor told me to stick my finger and test my blood once a month. There's only one problem. I don't have the machine I need. I'll get my doctor to write a Medicaid prescription for one."

"Grandma (Gary's mother) is diabetic and has a machine. I'm sure she'll let you use it," I said.

Pixie tested her blood sugar and the results were normal.

"She's not diabetic," my mother-in-law said. "I've had it up to here with her."

I called Pixie's doctor who confirmed that she didn't have diabetes. Pixie wore the arm bracelet for a week before trading it in for an arm sling, which was superior to the bracelet for attracting attention.

Meanwhile, Pixie nagged me into buying the karate suit for her and promised to pay me back when her Social Security disability check arrived.

She took one class before the operation.

Pixie came home from her karate class bouncing and excited. I greeted her at the door in a far more serious mood. I had checked her pillbox and found she hadn't taken any medicine for at least two days. I handed her the pills and a glass of water and watched her swallow them. Then I pointed out the house rules she had printed and posted in her room.

"You have broken two important house rules, *be honest* and *always do your best*. You told me you were taking your pills and you can't do your best without them. You can use the phone again in 24 hours." I checked the time.

Ten minutes later, Richard called. Pixie glared at me with murderous hatred while I took the message.

"It was Rick," I said.

"Who?"

"Richard. He was in the emergency room for chest pains again, but he's home now."

Pixie stomped outside to "check" on Alice and Ben.

Pixie liked being my "mother's helper," but Alice, annoyed with her daily visits to doctors and emergency rooms when nothing appeared wrong, refusal to take her medicine, and lying, was quickly losing respect for Pixie. Ben saw her as a playmate his own age. They thought of her as another child, not an adult, and neither would obey her. Pixie couldn't understand why she had lost the children's cooperation and was disturbed over it.

"Alice, Ben, it's time to come inside now," she yelled.

The kids were having a great time making mud pies and Alice threw a mud ball at Pixie. I held my breath and prayed, but to my relief, Pixie laughed and returned a mud ball herself. The game was afoot. The girls chased each other, threw mud, and laughed away the tension. Pixie helped Alice start her bath. When I went to remind Pixie to take her bath, I found her sound asleep with her feet hanging off the side of her bed. She was still wearing dirty clothes and her arm was caked with dried mud. The medicine had taken affect and caused her to fall into a deep sleep.

The next day I gave Pixie a half dose of medicine and watched to make sure she swallowed it. That day was lost to her. She spent it in a semi-awake, drugged state. It was clear her body wasn't used to the medicine.

I also made all her phone calls. Since there was a lot of last minute planning left before she went into the hospital, this punishment was as hard on me as it was on her. I wish I could tell you she learned the lesson, but she didn't. Both pill taking and lying continued being problems.

A few nights later I was working late, catching up with some writing after Ben and Alice fell asleep. Pixie stayed up to keep me company, although she was beginning to nod her head in a weak attempt to stay awake.

"It's 11:30. You look tired and need to go to bed. Your surgery is just two days away and you sure don't want to get sick now."

Just then the phone rang. Pixie answered it.

"It's Richard. He's in the hospital with chest pains and needs me there."

"That's the fourth time this week." I was beginning to think going to the emergency room in the middle of the night was Pixie and Richard's idea of a night out. They got attention and Medicaid paid the bill, which made it free in their eyes.

"I have to be with him."

"No, it's too late and your aren't feeling well yourself. I don't want you getting run down."

"I'll take my bike if you won't drive me."

"No, you need to get to bed. Richard will be fine."

She tried pouting. She tried crying. But I was firm. Pixie's maturity level was slipping rapidly.

"If I lived in the boarding home I could go. I told him I was coming."

"Call the hospital back and tell him you can't make it." She made a brief call. "He's not there. They sent him home without seeing him."

"You really care about Rick don't you?" I asked as I rubbed her back. Nightly reading and back rubs were something Ben and Alice always enjoyed and so did Pixie. Back rubbing relaxed her so she could sleep. It also was a way of communicating to her that I cared. I felt, if bonding was possible at all, it would take more than words for her to let down her wall and begin trusting, or loving, another person.

Almost three weeks passed from the time Pixie had moved in until she was well enough to have surgery. The night before Pixie's operation, I slept lightly. Sometime in the middle of the night Pixie woke up as a preschool aged child. She was scared and I sat with her until she fell back to sleep.

The hospital had asked Pixie to check in early. She brought along homework from her one day at high school and studied while we waited. This amazed me. Only the week before she had put on a big show about being unable to read or do math and now she was reading high school biology and trying to learn multiplication. After she grew tired of schoolwork, we talked.

When the nurse came to take blood, she calmly held out her arm, even though she claimed to be afraid of needles.

"I used to panic when anyone took my blood. It took four people to hold me down." Pixie loved talking about her misbehaviors.

"You're growing up now." The nurse taped a Band-Aid over the puncture wound.

Richard visited Pixie briefly. Later an elderly friend whom Pixie referred to as Grandma came. Pixie jumped into Grandma's lap, looking and acting like an oversized toddler. A minute later, she returned to adulthood and conversed with Grandma. She concentrated on her homework for a few minutes, and then began pacing back and forth like a caged tiger. When the stretcher was brought to take her into the operating room, Pixie climbed onto it. She was mute and frozen with fear. Grandma and I gave her one last hug before the attendant took her into surgery. I picked my kids up from school and went home to wait by the phone.

"Hello. This is Dr. James. Pixie did fine in surgery and will be out of recovery and back in her room in two hours. There were no gallstones, no ulcer. I took out her appendix to prevent any future problems with it, but I didn't find anything wrong to explain her stomach problems."

An hour later I returned to the hospital and was surprised to find Pixie already in her room. She was fully awake and had pulled the oxygen mask off her face in the recovery room. By the time I got there she was attempting to get up and walk to the toilet.

"Wait a minute, you're pretty shaky, let me call a nurse to help you," I said. Knowing how fearful she was of being alone, I stayed until visiting hours were over.

She called me in the middle of the night. "Mom, I hurt real bad."

"Did you tell your nurse?"

"Well, uh. I have to go now." She hung up.

I called the nurses desk and talked to the charge nurse who then gave Pixie a shot of pain medicine.

Pixie continued calling me every few hours all night long. The next day, still fighting anesthesia, pain, and hyperactivity, she was in and out of bed. She was still nauseated and I did my best to make her comfortable.

Grandma invited Pixie to stay at her house where it would be quieter than my active, child-oriented house. Pixie was upset that she had to do something that was difficult for her; she had to make a decision. She called me numerous times during the night to discuss where she should go. I told her she was welcome to come back but she had to decide for herself.

Pixie called early the next morning.

"I've been released. Come pick me up!"

She'd had exploratory surgery and an appendectomy only a day and a half earlier and the doctor had told her to expect a five-day stay. Since she couldn't settle down and rest, the hospital staff decided to release her early.

At home, Pixie watched television in the den. As weak as she was, she insisted on coming with me to pick-up the children from school. She was anxious to see them. Alice and Ben were glad she was home. They had missed her. When we returned home, I gave Pixie her medicine, but she refused to take it. She asked for the telephone, which I gave her. Then I went to sleep. She'd kept me up most of the past two nights.

Alice woke me. "There's a man in the house. Pixie let him in."

He was a CPS investigator from the adult abuse division. There'd been an abuse report saying I wasn't allowing Pixie to have her medicine and he was here to investigate.

"He told me Grandma called," Pixie whispered in my ear.

I knew that abuse investigators aren't allowed to disclose the source of the caller. I have a strong suspicion that Pixie was the caller, although she refused to admit it.

While I talked to the investigator, trying to clarify what had been going on, Pixie called her doctor and reported that she was having severe stomach pains. He told her to go to the emergency room. She spent the next six hours in Doctor's Hospital, but I didn't stay with her. I'd had enough of hospitals for a long time.

"She's a regular," one hospital employee told me on my way out. "Everyone in the hospital knows her and her boyfriend. One or the other comes to the emergency room at least three times a week. If they're busy, the doctors put them at the bottom of the list, so they usually leave before being seen."

It was past dinnertime before Pixie called for a ride home. The doctor told her she was fine and warned her not to over-exert herself.

When she arrived home, the neighbor's dogs were barking loudly and the noise upset her. I went across the street and asked them to quiet the dogs, to no avail. The neighbors, drunk and hostile, only encouraged the dogs to bark louder. The Pixie stood up, and although she could barely walk, somehow ran across the street. Soon she and my neighbors were in a verbal battle. Other people have told me that Pixie has a foul mouth, but I'd never heard her myself, and her language that night remained lady-like. The neighbor's language was not.

"I won't be talked to like that," Pixie said. She went into the house and called the police. This was already too much physical exertion for her, but when the police arrived, she insisted on going outside again, to talk to them. There was no reasoning with her.

The officers were less sympathetic. The neighbors had quieted their dogs as soon as the patrol car showed up, and the police discredited Pixie because they'd had problems with her in the past. She was shaking and clearly distraught. When the police were ready to leave, Pixie announced that she was in too much pain to move. The officer tried picking her up and carrying her into the house, but that created even more pain. Finally, I brought a chair from the house and they carried her inside while she sat on it.

Not more than ten minutes later, Grandma arrived. Pixie had called her after coming home from the hospital. I never found out what Pixie said to her, but like a raging storm, Grandma rushed into the house and escorted Pixie into her car. They left without saying goodbye. I was exhausted and my stomach was in an upheaval. Things hadn't been smooth, but they hadn't been that awful either. What a terrible way to end a friendship. "Are we ever going to see Pixie again?" Ben and Alice asked.

The next morning Pixie called.

"Will you be coming back?" I asked.

"No," she said in a distracted tone. I wasn't sure if she was talking to me, or someone at the house. "I'll call back later. Goodbye."

Later Grandma called. I could hear Pixie screaming in the background, "I'm going to Mom's if I have to walk."

I later learned that she walked several blocks to a convenience store before Grandma, fed-up and exhausted, brought her to my house.

Before Pixie arrived, we had a family meeting. In spite of her cheerfulness, no one was sure we wanted Pixie back. Her impulsive behavior, sudden anger, lies, and demands for constant attention upset everyone. She lived in the immediate and there was no waiting. Everything had to be done instantly. But we thought we knew her now and were better prepared to deal with her problems than we had been a few weeks earlier. We wanted another chance to make it work and finally decided she could return -- one more time.

When Grandma brought Pixie back, she had soiled pants and was using baby talk. I sent her inside to take a bath and go to bed. Grandma stayed awhile. We talked and a working relationship began. I sensed I had an ally in Grandma. Grandma had known Pixie since her early teens so she knew her history and abilities, as well as disabilities. After that day, I often called Grandma when I had questions and she was a great help.

The hospital had taken Pixie off all her medicines except the one for seizures.

"I'm not homicidal," Pixie said, "and I'm not suicidal, but the way I acted, Grandma could have called the police on me. I need to get back on my medicines. I hate the thought of going again, but it needs to be done in a hospital where they can monitor my blood levels." She spoke in an adult voice I'd never heard before. She made several phone calls to various hospitals and psychiatrists in town.

"Hi, this is Pixie," she said. They all knew her.

When talking to officials, she was at her most mature, adult level. She showed no signs of childishness or developmental delays. Within two hours she located a hospital with an open bed. The hospital was across town.

"It's late," I said. "Do you think you could wait until the morning? You could take one pill tonight."

"No, I really have to go tonight. They're holding the bed for me." Her mature voice and conversation made her argument sound reasonable. There was a sense of urgency in her request.

Looking back as I write this, I realize she was seeking a quiet place to recover from surgery. Just the thought of entering a psychiatric hospital would be traumatic to most people. But for Pixie, it's home.

"They need my social security card for identification or they won't accept me. Richard has it, so we have to go there first," she said.

"Why does she have your card?"

"I gave it to him to hold for me." Logic wasn't Pixie's strong suite.

"Rick's place is an extra half hour drive in the opposite direction. Is this absolutely necessary?"

Pixie is incredibly persistent, and believable when she puts her mind to it. Needless to say, I drove to Richard's only to find him gone.

"Now what?" I asked.

"Oh, don't worry. They'll let me in."

"How can you be so sure? You don't have the necessary I.D."

"Oh, I'll just tell them I'm suicidal," she laughed. "And if that doesn't work, I'll pitch a fit!"

Not only was Pixie manipulating me, she manipulated everyone, including professionals.

The psychiatric ward was locked. We rang the doorbell and a nurse unlocked the door, let us in, and then locked it behind us. The ward was quiet. The nurse's station was in the center of the floor facing the dayroom. There were tables, comfortable couches, padded chairs, and a large color television where the patients congregated. A hallway leading into the bedrooms surrounded the nursing station on the other three sides. There were free coffee and soda machines and telephones available for the patients' use.

Pixie went to the nurse's station to register. She answered questions and explained why she stopped taking her medications. She was an adult and showed no sign of regression. When asked the name of her caseworker, she hesitated, stuttered, and pretended to have forgotten Mary's name.

Why didn't she want Mary to know she was here? I wondered.

Then it was time for Pixie to sign herself in. She hesitated as she looked about the room. This was a new hospital that she had never been in before. Suddenly she slouched in her chair and began crying.

"What's the matter?" I asked.

"That chair. I won't be put in that chair." She pointed to a high backed geriatric chair sitting against the wall.

"Those chairs are only used for old people who are senile," the nurse explained. "You won't be put in one."

"I don't want to stay here." Pixie screamed. "I've been put in those chairs too many times. I want to go to another hospital."

It took a while to calm her down enough to sign the necessary papers. Her signature was loose and sloppy, resembling that of a child just learning to write.

At her insistence, Pixie was given a hospital bed.

The next day I brought her some clothes. As I entered the ward, two nurses were attempting to jerk Pixie to her feet. She resisted and cried out in pain.

"What's the matter?" I asked.

"It hurts," she answered in a whining, childish voice.

"Where does she need to go?" I asked the nurse. She pointed to the office.

I put my arm around Pixie and led her to the nurse's station. As usual, she responded well to my gentle encouragement.

The nurse needed her records. "Where has she been hospitalized before?"

Pixie gave them the names of every psychiatric hospital in town. This was her twelfth hospitalization this year.

I visited Pixie almost every morning while Ben and Alice were in school. The social worker greeted me one visit.

"Pixie has been *so bad.* She had to be put in the pink room three times."

"What's the pink room?"

"It's an empty, padded room where we put patients to calm down. It's painted pink, which is soothing. Pixie was lying on the couch exposed and refused to cover herself. When we told her to cover-up, she started screaming and cursing. It took four staff members to restrain her and she bit one," the social worker sighed. "Could you please bring her some clothes next time you visit?"

I was puzzled. *Why didn't the social worker know Pixie had clothes and why was Pixie's behavior so out of control?*

I went to her room to get her. Pixie was lying in bed, wearing two hospital robes, one tied in the front and one in the back. Her hair was stringy and unwashed and when I looked in the backpack for her hairbrush, I found her new toothbrush still in the wrapper. She silently glared at me. She'd been in the hospital only three days.

"I hate it here. A staff person threw me against the bed rail and it almost pulled out my stitches. He hurt my arm too. See? It's all swollen."

"Let me see. The stitches look okay. Your arm is swollen from the hospital I.V. You need to take a shower and get dressed. Then we can visit."

"Wearing clothes hurts my stitches."

"You can wear your new nightgown."

The nurse helped her shower and put on the pretty flannel gown before we went into the dayroom to visit. I had begun research for this book and the subject of substance-exposed babies interested Pixie. We talked about the physical features I had observed in my cocaine-exposed infants and she brought up the subject of the red birthmark on their necks.

"Can I look at your neck?" I asked, knowing her problems stemmed from alcohol, not cocaine. But there it was hidden under her hairline: a faded, penny-sized strawberry mark.

Lots of normal people have birthmarks, small eyes, or crooked toes. Alone, it doesn't mean anything. Also, many substance-exposed children don't have birthmarks or other features. But Pixie had a syndrome, a group of distinct features. She had several facial characteristics that by themselves mean nothing, but when combined, suggest Fetal Alcohol Syndrome. No one, even those with the most severe FAS, have all the possible features. Besides the facial features, Pixie was small, had signs of central nervous system damage including hyperactivity, slow learning, organically caused emotional disturbances, and her mother was a known alcoholic. There is no single test that can be given for Fetal Alcohol Syndrome or effect. It takes a specialist to diagnose it since other syndrome disorders such as Fetal Hydantoin (Meadows) syndrome and Noonan's syndrome have similar features. Children like Pixie are commonly found in foster care. Many of these children have experienced physical or sexual abuse and this, as well as long term foster care, can lead to serious emotional problems.

"Hi," I waved to the social worker as she walked past our table. She listened to Pixie discussing *I Would Be Loved*, which I had begun writing, and the problems substance exposed children experience.

"This is a side of Pixie we haven't seen before," the social worker told me later, referring to her mature, adult conversation and behavior. "I don't know anything about drug exposed babies. Is she right?"

"Yes, She knows more than she lets on."

The next day, the flustered social worker greeted me with another complaint. "We had to put Pixie in bed restraints last night, and then she called CPS to file an abuse report against the hospital. She says she was pushed against the bed rail and injured."

"She does that often. I heard she made a rape charge against the last hospital she was in."

"Was it true?"

"I don't know. CPS didn't find any evidence," I said.

"I don't know if she can be released with this behavior."

"She's here voluntarily to help regulate her medications. How's that going?"

"She's still on seizure medicine, but the doctor hadn't started anything else."

Four days had passed. Pixie was frustrated and so was I.

"You have to behave yourself," I told her. "If you continue acting crazy, they won't release you."

"Lies. Lies. Lies," a strange, angry voice screamed. Pixie had become another person, a stranger to me.

At that point, I decided I'd never take Pixie to another hospital. Pixie's caseworker, Mary, was encouraging me to help her stay in the community, so I thought this must be the correct decision. Neither Mary nor I realized how badly Pixie needed long-term hospital care. This led to a mistake I later came to regret.

The next time I visited, the neurologist was in Pixie's room attempting to get information about her seizures.

"I don't want to talk to him," came a babyish voice from under the bedcovers.

After a few questions, which I did my best to answer, Pixie removed the covers and began talking in her adult. She told him stories about her mother's seizures, as well as her sisters and brothers. She gave an amazing medical history about a family she'd never know and which I later learned included several imaginary people. Pixie described her own seizures, head banging, and hand shaking episodes in detail. Then she left her room to get the dinner she'd previously refused.

"Although seizures are common in people with FAS, I don't think she has them. That sound more like incidents related to her mental illness," the doctor confided.

The night before her release, the hospital had a Halloween party for the patients. Alice and Ben were invited and Pixie introduced them as her brother and sister. They were happy to see her again. Our house seemed quiet and lonely without her and they were looking forward to having her home. The kids had a great time playing games, and there was a buffet with sandwiches and cake. I visited with several patients who seemed normal. But not all did. Pixie's roommate was walking around yelling and hallucinating until she was finally put in the pink room. I also met King Henry the Eighth. It was a night to remember.

I WOULD BE LOVED
By Pixie

If I were a bird
I could fly high,

If I were a butterfly
I could fly high

If I were a dragonfly
I could fly high

But, most of all
If I were a puppy
I would be loved.

*Behavioral problems cause more difficulty for FAS
individuals than their level of functioning. Their behavior is
their biggest difficulty in managing life as an adult.*

LIFE ON A ROLLER COASTER

P ixie's doctor reduced her medication from eighteen pills a day to four. I was pleased, but I wouldn't have been if I'd know what was to come.

Pixie was released from the hospital the day her stitches were due to be removed, so we stopped at the medical doctors office on the way home. The doctor spent some time talking to her.

"The area around the wound is still weak and you must limit your activities for awhile. School is allowed, but you're not to do any strenuous activities. No bike riding for a couple weeks, and definitely no karate."

It was Halloween day when Pixie came home, feeling well and bouncing. We'd been planning her costume all month, but at the last minute she saw someone wearing a baby outfit that she liked better.

"I'd like to dress like a baby too," she said." "I'll wear my diapers and you can buy me a bottle."

Then Alice, who was overjoyed having her 'sister' home in time for Halloween, decided she wanted to be a baby too. The girls dressed in matching T-shirts, diapers, and pacifiers on a string around their necks. I refused to buy bottles. I remembered Ruth telling me Pixie still used a bottle at the age of seventeen and felt there was more than play in Pixie's desire for a baby costume. The kids went trick or treating.

"Twick or..." Pixie said.

"Tweet!" Alice chirped.

"Trick or treat -- smell my feet!" Ben yelled.

I laughed. I don't know who was having more fun, me or the kids. Soon their bags were loaded with candy.

"Pixie, you can help me carve the pumpkins into Jack-O-Lanterns." I handed her a sharp knife.

She glanced at the knife then looked away. "I don't know. I've never used a knife before -- appropriately."

"Appropriate," was one of her favorite words. All her life, people had told Pixie her behavior was inappropriate. When I asked her what the word meant, she defined it as "bad."

"No, you're not bad. You just have problems, but you can do this. I'll show you how." I wanted to teach her basic skills, and help her feel better about herself. With help, she hesitantly carved her first pumpkin.

"That's a great job. What a scary Jack-O-Lantern!"

The next morning, she insisted on riding her bike. Pixie lives for the moment and I couldn't stop her. She came back a few minutes later, white faced and exhausted. I knew keeping her quiet wasn't going to be easy. She bounced both physically and emotionally.

Monday morning Pixie was back in school but again, there were problems and she quit after one day. However, the law says disabled children have the right to attend public school until the age of twenty-one, and the school was obligated to educate her until then. Mr. Everglow suggested she try a special public school for severely disturbed children, as she couldn't function in the mainstreamed classes. Pixie needed to be evaluated and diagnosed Severely Emotionally Disturbed (SED). Then the school bus would pick her up for door-to-door service.

"I want to go but I can't sit quietly on the bus. They'll have to tie me in."

Pixie's self confidence was poor. She couldn't stay in school, sit still, keep friends, or even keep a family. There was so much she felt she couldn't do. I encouraged her as much as possible and tried teaching her new skills. I let her try cooking. Toasted cheese sandwiches seemed easy enough. Pixie turned the burner to high and scorched the first sandwich. With the stove still on high, she began burning the next. I had to intervene, giving her step-by-step directions. Pixie couldn't make the connection between the high flame and the burned sandwich. Pixie lacked cause and effect, the ability to understand how one thing leads to another. This mental process seems to be missing in many fetal alcohol exposed people, even when their intelligence on I.Q. tests is normal.

Pixie didn't understand why she had so much trouble. "I can't do anything right. I'm so stupid!" she yelled, running into her room.

We were frustrated. Neither Pixie nor I understood why she had this difficulty, although I suspected that the problems went deeper than either foster care of emotional disturbances.

That winter was colder than usual and our whole family caught colds. We had mild sore throats for a few days and then were better -- all except Pixie. She complained of a severe sore throat, which hurt for weeks. Even though her throat showed no sign of redness, she used a humidifier in her bedroom and went to the doctor or emergency room daily.

"I need a canister of oxygen," she said. "I can't breath."

I didn't seem properly concerned.

She was angry and continued her acting out. Everyday was something new.

"I left some things at the boarding home. I need to get my arm brace because my wrist hurts. It might be broken."

"You got everything when you left. Let me see your arm." I gave it a quick examination. There was no sign of injury or tenderness.

"No, the boarding home before there. I had to leave quickly."

When we arrived, Pixie was nervous. "Come in with me, please. I don't want any trouble."

The staff was friendly and we had no problems, but Pixie wasn't welcome back. She's monopolized the staff's time and attention until she was asked to leave. I carried out several large boxes of clothes -- more than she could possibly wear. She found a pair of crutches to play with, leaving me and the staff member to move everything for her.

All those clothes! Pixie had given me part of her disability check to help cover her cost of room and board but I'd spent every cent of that money buying her new clothes. I was steaming. Alice was angry too, but Pixie got into her good graces by sharing the wardrobe. Pixie wore the same size as my nine-year-old daughter.

Pixie wanted my full attention twenty-four hours a day, so I had to set limits. From dinner until bed was Ben and Alice's special time with me. After the children were asleep, it was Pixie's time. She was a night owl and so am I. I love the house in the evening when all is quiet and dark. It was my favorite time to think and it was the time when Pixie talked to me.

"I'm glad I found my baby bottle in the box," she said. "I need it."

"I have no objections to you having a bottle, but only water. I don't want your teeth to rot." I knew I would lose if I objected, but I wanted to discourage such infantile behavior.

"I suppose Alice will tease me."

"I suppose you're right. I think you should keep it private."

"Okay," she said. She filled the bottle with water, lay on the couch and sucked it in front of me. I went to bed. That took the fun out of it. The next week, when I offered to buy her a new music tape in exchange, she hesitantly gave the bottle up. It wasn't an easy

decision, and it took her three days to make it. She chose a tape called *Silly Children's Songs*. I didn't mind. She had taken a big step towards growing up. She listened to her music tapes and sang along. She learns songs quickly and has a natural ear for music.

Going from a baby to an adult, Pixie resumed her GED classes at her daycare. Like many fetal alcohol exposed children, Pixie struggled with math. She had trouble with multiplication and abstract thinking as well as cause and effect. During the day she went to classes and in the evening she studied. Because this was important to her, she was able to sit long enough to do her assignments. Deep in concentration, she looked like any normal teenager. But she wasn't.

One characteristic of FAS, which plagues Pixie, is her impulsiveness. I never knew when she would lose control. One quiet Saturday afternoon, Pixie asked me to take her to the toy store. There were some things she wanted to look at for Christmas. I thought she wanted to buy gifts for Ben and Alice and didn't realize she intended to look for gifts only for herself. She walked around the store acting very adult until we entered the doll department.

"I really like this doll. Can I buy it?"

"It's too expensive. You'll have to save your money."

"But I want it *now,*" Pixie said in her baby voice.

"Why don't you think about it overnight?" You can come back and buy it another day."

"No. Why can't I? I want it *right now,*" she stamped her foot.

I decided we'd better leave the store immediately. A temper tantrum was brewing.

I've gone through this before with Tara, Rosey, and LaKeisha. I expect they will outgrow such actions, but will they? Foster care, moving from home to home, neglect, beatings, and sexual abuse. Is this the outcome? I put my arm around Pixie's shoulders and guided her outside. To my relief, she followed without resistance. Again, Pixie responded well to a gentle approach.

At home, baby Pixie brought up the subject of the doll again.

"Why can't I have it?" she whined.

"We will talk about it later."

"I want to talk about it now."

"We can discuss it when you are ready to be an adult."

"Humph," she said and stormed into her room.

We did discuss it later. She wanted a baby doll and planned taking it out in public. I also discussed the incident with her psychiatrist who felt it would encourage inappropriate behavior. There would be no doll.

Pixie soon forgot about the doll. Despite her problems, we had many good times. Alice considered Pixie her best friend and I think the feeling was mutual. Often in the evening, Ben, Alice, Pixie and I walked to the store for a snack. Pixie was having less trouble eating and was also taking her seizure medicine without reminding, although I checked her pillbox daily to make sure.

This seemed a happy time in Pixie's life, and she told me stories late into the evenings. The stories, however, were tragic.

"I once was friends with a normal girl in school. She could sit still through class, and she never got in any trouble. Oh, I wanted to be like her. I really tried but I just didn't know how...

"When I lived in an institution, I used to break windows with my hands. I don't do that anymore, it's too painful."

Pixie is a master storyteller, weaving truth with fantasy and exaggeration. But there *was truth* in her stories and it was like peeling the layers of an onion. With each layer removed, there were tears. I never cried aloud, in front of her, but my heart ached for her. There were stories about beatings, incest, and rape. She talked about her suicide attempts, the alcohol related death of her mother, and a friend's death.

There was one happy story: "Mary, my caseworker at the daycare, is buying me a new bike for staying out of the hospital a whole month. She's not counting the time I went in to regulate my meds. I'm getting it next week."

Now I knew why she hadn't wanted Mary to know about her most recent hospitalization.

Pixie's moods jumped up and down more often now. One minute she was an adult, the next a young child. She was silly and happy, and she was angry. Back and forth. Up and down. She danced and sang along with children's music tapes.

"Boom, boom, ain't it great to be crazy," she sang in a childish voice. "No, it's not," she interrupted in her serious adult speech. "Boom, boom..." she continued with the song, again a child. Pixie's mood was infectious. We all were acting a bit crazy. Joking, I checked to see if the moon was full.

She was silly – much too silly – and some of her behavior was alarming. She grabbed the kitten by its tail and swung it. Pixie loved animals and had always been gentle with my pets.

Pixie, who rarely watched anything on television but cartoons, overheard a news report. A woman had slashed her children's throats and cut her own wrists. She was recovering in a psychiatric hospital. Pixie was fascinated. For days afterwards, she talked about appropriate and inappropriate uses of knives.

People who have heard this story ask me why I didn't get rid of Pixie then and there. I seriously thought about it, but it was as though I had gotten on a roller coaster ride. There is nothing difficult about getting into the car before it's actually moving. Then the roller coaster starts moving slowly up the hill. *This isn't so bad.* After awhile, it stops at the top. I look around and see the beautiful scenery. *A bit high but look at those lovely trees.* Then there's the drop, but not until it's over do you see the whole picture.

This is where we were, at the top, just about ready for the fall. But like a roller coaster, once we got on, there was no getting off. And like a roller coaster, the really exhilarating parts were over very quickly and then we *could* get off. What happened next is difficult to put into print. The memory is painful for me. It's like describing the sudden fall at the end of the ride.

The last week Pixie stayed with us, Alice had an out of town sports competition two hours away. The whole family went and Pixie offered to help watch Ben. Ben wasn't interested in seeing the competition and Pixie couldn't sit still for more than a few minutes. They played together throughout the long day while Gary and I enjoyed watching Alice. Afterwards, we went out to eat. The kids were happy but their behavior was wild and the word crazy was brought up several times in the conversation. It seemed "appropriate." The drive home was long and everyone was tired. Gary drove, Alice sat in front between Gary and me, while Pixie and Ben played in the back seat.

"How much longer?" Pixie asked.

There was an urgent plea to her question, conveying she needed to be home. It had been a long day -- too long for her. She began throwing clothes over Ben's head and laughing.

"You're getting too wild. Calm down!"

Her loss of control was frightening and her wild behavior continued escalating. Soon she was laughing so hard she threw her head against the back seat and then against the front, rocking wildly. I grabbed her head, held her still and forced eye contact.

"Calm down, Pixie!"

Suddenly Pixie was not only calm, she was gone. She was mute, gently rocking, staring out the window with glazed, unseeing eyes. It was as though her soul had left her body. Alice, Ben and I took turns talking to her in a soothing voice, rubbing her back, and singing her favorite songs – but she wasn't there.

When we arrived home, she sat alone in the car until I took her hand and led her into the house. I guided her to her room and into bed. Once in bed, she began rolling her arms back and forth in a violent, shaking motion.

Is this a seizure? I wondered. When I tried talking to her, she began kicking her feet and screaming. I left her alone; attempts to calm her only made matters worse. Eventually she calmed down, curled into a fetal position, and sucked her thumb until she fell asleep.

Alice and Ben played in quiet whispers at the far end of the house. It was a frightening experience for us all.

Half an hour later, Pixie came out of her room.

"Welcome back," I said.

"What are you talking about and when did we get home?"

"We've been home about an hour. What happened to you?"

"I fell asleep. I think."

I described what had occurred and she was worried it might happen again, but she seemed all right for the moment.

"It had been a long day and Alice slept in my room.

"I think Pixie needs to have a room alone tonight," she said with sensitivity beyond her years. As it turned out, she was correct.

Pixie stayed up later than the children and over the next three hours her excitement escalated. I called her doctor and he called the pharmacy for a prescription, which she refused to take. She was out of contact with reality and sang, "Pecan pie, pecan pie," over and over at the top of her voice, and tried putting a dead grasshopper, which normally frightened her, down my back. Her conversation jumped from one subject to another and made no sense. She talked in a loud, rapid voice about the woman who cut her children's throats. Soon her hands began shaking out of control as though she were trying to release all the pent up energy from the past few days. To reduce stimulation, I turned off the lights, closed the door, and left her alone to recover.

Her desperate need for quiet isn't any different from my other foster children who were substance exposed. Like Sammy and Jasmine, she needs time away from all stimulation, I thought.

After a few minutes, she calmed down enough to be taken to bed and given medicine. She again rolled up in a fetal position, sucked her thumb, and whimpered.

Such a broken little girl. How can I help ease your hurt?

I called her psychiatrist and talked to him. After the last miserable time, I didn't want her back in the psychiatric hospital -- a terrible mistake I soon came to regret. He said she could be left to sleep through the night, but if she hadn't recovered in the morning, I would have no choice but to take her to the hospital. I didn't expect her to wake up but I hid my knives just in case. I had hidden all the medicine a week before, after she told me about her suicide attempt through a drug overdose.

The next day the kids made every attempt to be as quiet as possible. I gave Pixie her medicine and she spent much of the day sleeping. She was calm, and regressed to a two-year-old level. Later in the evening she regained her adult persona and seemed to have completely recovered. It would be four more days until her doctor could see her and evaluate her medication. As usual, Pixie resisted taking her antipsychotic medicine that took away the voices whispering in her head.

Pixie was a different person now. The smiling child listening to silly children's songs, and singing along, gave way to an angry, upset, and impulsive young lady. All joy left her.

She began attending a new daycare program for emotionally disturbed adults. Patty, a friend of hers, was going there also.

"We lived in the same abusive foster home," Patty mimed hair pulling.

"See, I told you she pulled our hair. I wasn't lying!" Pixie exclaimed.

Patty seemed more mature than Pixie, although she'd also been raised in foster care and had emotional problems similar to Pixie's. Together they were like two ten-year-olds. The next time I met Patty the tables were turned, she was acting like an immature child and Pixie was the adult one. Patty bounced ages too.

Is this the outcome when our government raises children? Is it the result of prenatal exposure to drugs? Or is it a combination of all the suffering Pixie and Patty have experienced in their short lives?

I met with the director of the daycare. While we talked, Pixie joined the group of young adults. We watched the young men vying to gain Pixie's attention, and spoke about her sexual immaturity – she seemed so innocent, so naïve.

"All hell will break loose when she becomes sexually active," the director predicted.

"I expect that will be quite a long time off. She doesn't show any signs that she is aware of her sexuality."

"You never know with these kids. They can learn about sex faster than you'd imagine. When she does, there are going to be big problems."

Just then, Pixie interrupted our conversation. "Patty wants to move in with us. She isn't happy where she lives now. We could make your office into her bedroom."

I laughed, *Pixie and Patty – forever children.*

"No. We don't have room," I said, "and I need my office for writing."

Pixie demanded my undivided devotion and was jealous when I gave my own children attention. One like her was all I could handle.

Later, when I saw Patty have a temper tantrum, I knew I'd made the right decision.

"Her behavior was terrible," Pixie said, not realizing how similar Patty's conduct was to her own. "I want nothing more to do with her."

These foster children hold deep anger which boils very close to the surface and, like a volcano, they can – and do – erupt without reason or warning, I thought.

Pixie wanted a puppy. Over the weekend she brought home a black lab mix from a neighbor's litter.

"He's free. Can I keep him, please?" She flashed her most charming smile and looked directly in my eyes. Her small, widely set teeth helped complete the picture of an innocent child. "I'll take care of him. You won't have to do a thing."

"How can you take care of a puppy? You can't even take care of yourself," I said. "I have an idea. I know someone who has a newborn litter of puppies. You can pick one out and if you can prove to me that you can take care of yourself, you may have it when the puppy is weaned."

I made a chart to help Pixie remember to take her medicine and do her self-care skills including bathing, brushing her hair and teeth. She was earning a puppy.

"It's no fair," she complained often. "Alice doesn't have to keep a chart."

"It's no fair," Alice complained. "Pixie gets to stay up late."

It was no fair. Alice had been born healthy. She had a loving mother and father and a nice home with every advantage that we could afford to give her. Pixie had none of this and never would. And it was no fair that Pixie jealously demanded all my time and attention for herself. Alice needed me too, and so did Ben. Pixie's intense anger exhausted not only me, but Gary and the children as well.

"No fair," was becoming the complaint of the day. This reminded me of a favorite story, which I told the girls:

"Once upon a time there was a mother and a father and they had a son named Bobby who was ten years old. Then they had another child. A baby girl. They wanted to be fair, so they named the baby Bobby Two. Because Bobby Two was a baby, she had to sleep in a crib, wear diapers, and drink from a bottle. The parents wanted to be fair, so they made their son, Bobby One, also sleep in a crib, wear diapers, and drink from a bottle.

'It's no fair,' Bobby One said.

"The mother and father didn't understand. They thought they were being fair because they gave their children the same name and treated them identically. They had treated their children equally, but equal isn't always fair."

"I'm being fair to you both, just not equal," I said. "You each have different needs. Pixie needs a chart and Alice needs to go to bed early."

The girls understood and the competition became less intense, for a while.

One aspect of Pixie's behavior that concerned me since the day she'd worn only a towel in front of Richard was her lack of modesty. She seemed to be at the same sexual developmental level as Ben. Like him, she knew she needed to keep her clothes on, but this was something she did because she had learned it, not because she had any true feelings of modesty. At times, she exposed herself inappropriately.

I asked her psychiatrist about this. "It seems to me Pixie has decided to stay a child and this includes refusing to grow up sexually. I wonder if it could be a response to the sexual abuse she experienced as a baby and throughout childhood?"

"That's a possibility. She was badly abused on several different occasions. I suggest you tell her whenever her behavior is inappropriate."

Although Pixie acted sexually innocent, she had a lovely figure and often wore tight clothes. The young men around her couldn't fail noticing this. The emotionally disabled men in her daycare center competed for her attention.

I'd heard her mention several boyfriends and told Pixie I would like to meet her friends. She could invite them to an activity. I always looked for programs to take my children to on weekends, and this week a children's play was being performed. Alice, Ben, and Pixie all looked forward to our outings. She invited Mike and Alfred from her daycare. They met us at the theatre but since it would be dark before the play was over, I'd agreed to drive them home. Mike was a nice looking young man. He seemed normal in both appearance and conversation. However, he had used illegal drugs as a teenager, which had damaged his brain. Alfred though, was abnormal appearing. His head was small and his eyes were wide-set like Pixie's. His conversation led me to believe he was slow mentally.

The play was terrific, everyone had a great time and was in high spirits. On the way home, the conversation in the car became silly and wild. Remembering another car ride, I told Pixie and the boys to calm down. To my relief, she responded without any problem.

"That was a great night, even Pixie behaved herself," Alice said. I realized we'd all begun having reservations about Pixie. The early fun had become tension filled. Having her around now was like playing catch with a bomb – we remained on guard waiting for an explosion. Tonight had been a treat though.

Later that evening, looking past me at the wall in her bedroom, Pixie began talking.

"I liked that play, and the chairs were comfortable. But I don't like the geriatric chairs in the hospital. When they put me in one, my arms are restrained at my side and I can't move. If they leave my feet free, then I can kick – but they'll restrain my feet if I do. It's not like being alone – there are crazy people all around. Some can be violent and attack. There's no way I can defend myself in the chair. I'm helpless. The pink room is nicer. It's safe there. I'm all alone where no one can hurt me. I look around and all I see is pink. I look at those pink walls and begin feeling so calm and relaxed. And then I'm okay again."

That week I could have painted the whole world pink but Pixie still wouldn't have been okay. The doctor still hadn't evaluated her medications. She refused to take what she had in the house and had been off most of her medicine for too long. She was becoming seriously ill.

Feeling moody and depressed, she returned from the daycare full of stories. "I have a terrible time riding my new bike. I can't manage the brakes. You'll have to drive me from now on."

"You've been doing fine riding your bike." Now that Pixie was feeling better, I wasn't anxious to continue as her personal chauffeur.

"Today I almost fell down in front of a car. Then the bike got stuck on the railroad track and a train was coming. I barely got off in time. After that, a dog chased me and bit me on the leg."

"Let me see the bite," I said.

"He really just bit my pants cuff. Here, see it? He almost tore it, too." She lifted the cuffs to show me, but there was no tear.

"What a liar," Alice whispered. "Does she really expect us to believe her?"

"Now you know why it's important to always tell the truth," I whispered back.

"I forgot to tell you," Pixie continued. "My counselor said I need a coloring book. Can you get me one? I told her when I get mad I think about jumping in front of a car and killing myself. Then a minute later I don't even remember why I was so angry. She told me I should go into my room and color when I feel like that."

Pixie's anger had the strength of a volcano building toward an explosion. Life was falling apart for her. She flushed the medicine prescribed to stabilize her mood swings down the toilet when I tried giving her one.

I felt uncomfortable letting her ride the bike but she needed to work off her excess energy, so I could only hope she was able to keep herself safe. The director of her daycare had told me that, in spite of her threats, Pixie wasn't suicidal. I hoped she was right.

"Can I trust you to ride your bike safely or do you need me to drive you today?"

She looked at me with hatred in her eyes, "Are you asking if I'm suicidal?"

"Are you?"

"Do I look suicidal?" she chewed her already over bitten fingernails.

"I don't know. *Are you?*"

She gave me one last glare as she left on the bike. My stomach hurt the rest of the day. I didn't think my health could stand much more of this, but I couldn't get off the roller coaster, the ride hadn't finished quite yet. I had come to care very much for Pixie and couldn't just dump her onto the streets. I would have to see it through to the end.

That evening, Pixie continued making suicidal threats. I spent hours talking with her until she calmed down and climbed into bed. Although she was unwashed and her filthy clothes had not been changed for days, I breathed a sigh of relief. We'd made it through another day.

Alice had been wonderful. She helped Ben get to bed, did her homework without being told, took her bath, and was in bed waiting for her good-night kiss. I went to talk to her and tell her how proud I was. It was hard believing this was the same child who, just a few months earlier, had required hours of nagging to do a simple homework assignment. Alice was learning to handle difficult situations in her life, and becoming a kind, sensitive person. I could see that both my children were becoming stronger, better people.

Pixie's boyfriend, Richard, introduced me to his sister. We discussed the effects an emotionally disturbed child has on their siblings.

"I don't think having a disabled sibling hurt me," she said. "It made me a more sensitive person. Your kids will be fine."

My kids were.

Pixie cuddled our cat until it jumped off the bed and ran from her. She'd pulled its tail and then began crying.

"Go to her, Mom," Alice said.

"What's the matter, Pixie?"

"The cat scratched me – here," she pointed to her eyebrow.

I put antibiotic cream on the non-existent scratch and went back to Alice. Pixie had staged the scene because she didn't want to share my attention. She had to learn that Alice and Ben needed me too.

After that, not a day went by without Pixie pulling at least one stunt, and each day she surpassed the previous. Crying and suicide threats gave way to lying on the floor and kicking, head banging, and calling the police. The children and pets avoided her, while Gary and I discussed finding another home for her – but where? We decided to wait until she saw her doctor and restarted the medicine. It was only a few days away and might make a difference.

Five days had passed since our disastrous out-of-town trip. I took Pixie to her doctor's appointment. I'd learned he could administer Pixie's antipsychotic medicine through a monthly intramuscular injection rather than the hated pills. I'd discussed this shot with Pixie earlier. She'd agreed at the time but I never knew when she would change her mind. I expected her doctor to start the medicine immediately.

We had a short wait and Pixie spent the time screaming at everyone around her. Finally, her doctor called me into his office while Pixie waited outside.

Pixie's file, set on the doctor's desk, looked like a thick book. "There must be over three hundred pages," I said.

"This is volume two," the doctor told me. "Her problems are not only from the trauma of abuse and foster care. She has brain damage. There's not much anyone can do about that, but drugs can help her function and reduce the drastic mood swings."

I heard Pixie screaming through the door.

"I want her to get the medicine intramuscularly. She won't take the pills."

"If she agrees, I can make her an appointment to get the shot. It's given at the clinic once a week."

Then it was Pixie's turn to talk to the doctor. I could hear her screaming through the door. "My medicine is none of her business. I can manage it myself."

Oh, little girl, I wish you could. I don't like this anymore than you do.

Pixie agreed to take the injection starting the next week.

"In the meantime," the doctor said, "start taking the pills again."

"Fine," said Pixie. "But I won't take them from *her.*"

I knew she wouldn't take them at all.

That afternoon I took Alice and Ben with me to run some errands. For the first time, Pixie decided to stay home alone.

"I'll be all right," she promised. "My counselor is picking me up in half an hour. I'll be with her."

Alice, Ben, and I enjoyed out time out. We looked in the pet store and the kids got sample cookies from the grocery. We spent our afternoon enjoying being together. We could relax and breath freely for the first time in what seemed a long while. That last week had felt more like a year.

We arrived home after Pixie did. She ran out of the house sobbing in fear. She grabbed me around the waist and hung on. It took some time to comfort her. If Pixie couldn't stay alone for an hour, how could she *ever* become self-sufficient or learn to live on her own? I couldn't put her out.

By now, Pixie was angry and demanding almost constantly. She wore her CRABBY T-shirt for days at a time, refused to bathe, and ordered everyone around. There was no pleasing her.

"You always put your kids first. You love them more."

Ben had a tiny room of his own, no bigger than a walk-in closet, and Pixie wanted it.

"I'll ask the kids if they mind moving." The kids *did* mind moving. Ben didn't want to give up his room, and Alice didn't want to share her room with a "yucky boy."

"I have no privacy."

"If you go into the room and close the door, nobody will bother you."

"I'm leaving. I'm going to Grandma's or to the hospital. *I won't stay here another night.*"

Grandma said no.

Pixie called the psychiatric hospitals. She spent the next two hours explaining to mental health professionals how terribly she was being treated and how the stress of living here was making her suicidal.

I read to Ben and Alice and got them ready for bed. We all tried ignoring Pixie, but none of us could. I felt angry, worried, confused. The kids were upset and the household was filled with tension. We were over our heads and I knew it, but I still was reluctant to see another hospitalization. It hadn't even been two weeks since the last one.

The next morning Pixie was all ready to move into Ben's room. I tried stalling her. I knew from experience that she rarely followed through on things she started and could usually be distracted. With luck, her mood would change and she would forget about it. Pixie has a poor memory for most things, but once she gets an idea firmly in her mind, she doesn't forget.

When I refused to help her, she took Ben's belongings out of his room and threw them on the guest bed in Alice's room. Then she took her things into Ben's room. Alice and Ben were furious. Gary and I were at a loss about what to do. Pixie had changed from a sweet child into an angry, manipulative and unpredictable nightmare. Her behavior had become so disruptive that we felt any change had to be an improvement, so we decided to allow the move to stand. If Pixie were happier in her own room then everyone's life would be calmer.

We were all walking on eggshells, careful not to upset her before she started the intramuscular medication. Then, I believed, everything would be all right again. It was just a few days more until we would have our cheerful Pixie back.

It was this thought that kept me from throwing her out onto the streets then and there.

Pixie demanded I drive her to daycare at the same time my children had to be picked up from school. A fact she knew.

"Your case manager, Mary, gave you bus tickets to get there," I reminded her.

"I can't walk in that neighborhood. I was raped there," she yelled, storming out of the house.

Hurricane Pixie swirled through my life. Like the center of the storm, I appeared calm, but my chewed fingernails and frequent stomachaches told a different story.

Her counselor came to the house to talk to her.

"Pixie seems happy. I think this placement is working," the counselor told me.

"I'll need a therapist myself if she stays much longer. I'm having serious doubts about my ability to manage her without professional support. I need to consider my children's mental health as well as mine.

"I'll look into it but I can't promise anything. Our funding is limited to direct services for our clients. We don't supply help for the families," the counselor said.

Later Pixie came with me to pick the kids up from school and then walked to the bus stop. She was going to her GED class and then her respite worker would bring her home.

I was glad Pixie had respite. It gave us a regular break from each other and I appreciated this service. Like everything else, Pixie seemed to take it for granted without showing much gratitude. But although she couldn't show it outwardly, I knew the respite was as important to her as it was to us.

Pixie returned home and helped put the kids to bed. She was delightful – playful, but controlled. She seemed more at ease having her own room and went to bed early.

"Good night, Mom."

"Good night," I kissed her cheek. "I love you."

"I love you, too."

I wondered. *Can she love?*

A few minutes later she came out crying. "The cat *really* scratched me this time," she admitted the previous evening's fakery.

"Let me see." The scratch was so small I had to squint to see it. I knew the gentle cat wouldn't scratch without a reason.

"That's terrible! Call the ambulance. The doctors will probably have to cut your arm off." I teased.

Pixie laughed and we started roughhousing. She was small and not especially strong, so it amazed me that it had taken four people to restrain her at the hospital.

Her happiness with the new room didn't last long. Pixie woke in a hostile mood. Without her medicines, her thoughts raced like a wheel spinning on ice.

"I think I'm having an appendicitis," she said.

"Your doctor removed your appendix during the surgery."

"I could be dying and you don't even care."

Looking at her, I saw no sign of pain in either her movements or her voice. It was clear she was trying to manipulate me into driving her somewhere. Anywhere.

"Call the doctor," I said.

"The doctor isn't in," she slammed down the phone.

I listened to her yell and decided it was time to tackle her anger head on. I'd previously warned her she'd be sent to her room for any more inappropriate behavior.

I put my arm around her shoulder. "You need to lie down now."

"No, I don't," she continued arguing while I guided her into her bedroom like I would a young child. I closed the door but I could hear her crying. A few minutes later she came out of her room with her composure regained, as though nothing had happened. Later I asked her if she understood why she had been sent to her room and she answered "no."

That evening, when it was time to put the children to bed, Pixie wanted to go to the emergency room. I refused. This was the kids time, not hers. She tried Gary, and he also refused, saying that he couldn't see anything wrong.

A moment later, Pixie has a rip-roaring *temper tantrum*. She began crying and pounding her head against the door as hard as she could. I had thought there was nothing more Pixie could do to surprise me but I was unprepared for the violence she displayed. When I realized she was serious about injuring herself, I restrained her in my arms until she was calm enough to safely release.

Late that night, Pixie began complaining again. She was still active and not showing any behavior suggesting the need for medical care. Eventually she called a Medicaid cab to give her a ride to the hospital, at taxpayer's expense.

She returned home at three in the morning. I was sleeping fitfully and woke up when she came in.

"The doctor said I may have torn the stitches internally from riding the bike too soon. I need to see my doctor and have

X-rays. You should have driven me. I was in so much pain." She looked at me with a devilish smile, but her eyes glared with anger.

The next day I took Pixie to the adult daycare center.

"We're going to the park. Would you mind driving?" the activities leader asked me.

I was able to fit seven adults into my full sized station wagon, but the car rode low to the ground.

They were an incongruous lot: Pixie was angry and sulking, Patty was happy and childish, Mike and Alfred were competing for Pixie's attention. One man was arguing with an imaginary adversary. Several had odd facial features, although others seemed normal in appearance and behavior. Never one to be shy, I asked how many had ever been in foster care. Five of the seven had.

Pixie ran and played in the park. Her severe pain from the previous night was forgotten. She never did follow-up with her doctor. The trip to the emergency room seemed to have cured her pains, if not her mood.

Pixie was scheduled for the intramuscular medication – just one more day to get through. I knew her nasty mood revolved, to a great degree, around the fact she had taken no medication at all for at least a week and had not been on the correct medications and dosage for several months. I was optimistic. Tomorrow, after the injection, Pixie would again be pleasant and sane.

That afternoon Pixie took the bus to see her case manager. She called and asked me to drive her to a senior citizen's boarding home that had an opening.

Angry, I refused to take her, "If you're going to move out, then you can arrange your own transportation. I'm busy." I'd made plans to spend the afternoon with my kids and I wasn't going to let her ruin it.

That afternoon there was a heavy rainstorm with thunder and lightening. Rain was pouring in sheets. Pixie talked an acquaintance into taking her to the boarding home on his motorcycle so she could fill out an application. Her powers of manipulation and her impulsiveness required everything be done the instant the thought occurred to her, as though it were a matter of life or death. She came home soaking wet, sulking, and silent.

The next day Pixie was scheduled to get her injection and as far as I was concerned, it came none too soon. Mike, Pixie's friend from the day care and theatre, was there waiting for his shot. Pixie was so restless she could barely talk. She yelled at no one in particular. I'd never seen her so agitated. Finally her name was called.

"Did it hurt?" I asked when she came out.

"No." She smiled. "I didn't get it. I told them I was allergic to the other medicine so they're giving me pills to try for a month before giving me the medicine in a shot."

Mike later told me I became a ghost white.

She can't come back to my house, was all I could think.

The boarding home she'd applied to the day before had an opening and I helped her move out. Her new roommate was ninety years old.

"You're always welcome back to visit. You haven't burned your bridges, " I said. "But you can't ever live here again."

We stayed in touch and Pixie visited a few times. Six weeks and three moves later, I got a phone call from her.

"Mom, can I come back home? I've been raped."

Pixie had begun taking the medicine. *Maybe, this time we can make it work,* I thought as I climbed back onto the roller coaster. *She has nowhere else to go.*

*Alcohol is a teratogen, a substance that causes birth defects.
The word teratogen comes from the Greek word "terrat" which
means "monster." Hence, teratogen means, "to make
monsters."*

TROUBLED ANGELS

Although the story of my foster children must come to a close, their stories continue without me, and I know little of them.

I learned Valentine had her tonsils and adenoids removed and tubes put in her ears, but she continued getting sick. A year later she went home with her birth mother. I don't know if she was able to stay with her family or not. Many children return to foster care repeatedly, and I suspect she will be one of them. The last time I heard anything about Valentine, immunology specialists at Children's Hospital were studying her. The experts were still puzzled.

However, I have an idea as to what the problem may have been. Several months after she left my care I was watching a television show on about Fetal Alcohol Syndrome. There was a description of an FAS child: the small wide set eyes, flattened upper lip, poor growth, delayed language, and bonding or attachment difficulties. As far as knew, I'd never seen a young child with Fetal Alcohol Syndrome before, but when the television showed a picture of a child with this disorder, I turned on the VCR and ran to get my photo album. I froze the picture of the FAS child on the screen and next to it I placed Valentine's picture. There is no doubt that there was a strong resemblance. These two children could have been twins.

After Woody went home, his mother and I kept in touch for a while. He continued improving and his stiffness subsided until he could relax his body when someone held him. For the first time, he could cuddle. He mastered crawling and walking along furniture. As he stood up more, his feet began straightening and he learned to walk. He was slow talking and didn't say his first word until he was two. At two years old he was ambidextrous and used both hands equally well, but rarely together. Most babies are clearly left or right handed before this age.

Woody has come a long way, but he still has a rough road ahead of him. Learning to read and keeping up with unimpaired children will be a challenge when he reaches school age. But for now, few people notice the slight tightness and his fisted hands. What everyone notices is Woody's wonderful, expressive eyes, and happy smile. He has the personality of a winner!

Woody now has a baby sister. She was born full term and drug free.

I still regret that I wasn't able to keep Tara, my little redheaded terror, for six more weeks. During that time she was removed from three more foster homes and CPS decided not to return her to her mother. They felt her mother wouldn't be able to handle her.

While I was in the process of writing this chapter, I received a fortuitous phone call. Apparently my phone number was still in Tara's file and a secretary or nurse in a doctor's office called me by mistake. I inquired about Tara.

Tara had been placed in the Children's Home, a local orphanage-like facility and treatment center where CPS places children who are too emotionally disturbed to live with a family. By the time she was old enough to attend kindergarten, Tara was back in foster care, taking medicine to help calm her down. There were no plans at that time for reuniting her with her mother or for adoption.

I never saw Rosey after she went home on that happy Christmas day. However, my friend Dianne met her in a shopping mall about six months later. She was with a woman who was not her mother, and there were several other children of various races with them. Apparently, she's back in foster care.

Sammy, Jasmine the Screamer, and Heather, the alert infant who stayed only one week with me, left and I have never heard another word. I hope they are all right.

I haven't heard from LaKeisha either. LaKeisha, like Rosey, will probably end up living in a facility for the developmentally disabled. I don't believe either one has much chance of ever finding a stable family.

Less than a week after Pixie left my house for the senior citizens boarding home, she was hospitalized. Then she moved to another boarding home – one with younger clientele, and met the boy she claimed raped her. I let her move back into my house but she was hospitalized again the next day. Shortly after that she used her newly learned karate skills on a police officer and landed in jail for a week.

Her chaotic life continued until she was finally committed to the state psychiatric hospital. Although there was no rehabilitation there that met her needs, it was a wonderful place for her. Out in the country, miles away from the nearest town, she had freedom to walk outside. There was a school where she studied for her GED and worked in a green house. She went on field trips to town. At night, she was safely locked inside her cottage. Here was the structure and professional staff she needed. Pixie stayed there three years, on and off, until the hospital closed and patients were put out on the street with little follow-up care.

Ten years later, Pixie is still homeless, still moving from friend to friend. However, it's gotten much harder now.

Pixie has three young children – a future generation of foster children to carry on the legacy.

"Everyone has hopes which they keep in a
special place. I keep my hopes on the stars."
--Ben Falkner (age 6)

EMBRACING THE FUTURE

Approximately one child in every 750 to 1,000 births has Fetal Alcohol Syndrome. Probably twice that number are born with Fetal Alcohol Effect. We can only guess how many children have learning or emotional problems because they were exposed to alcohol before birth. Women who use cocaine, heroin, or other illegal drugs during their pregnancy frequently use alcohol as well. An estimated 100,000 to 375,000 children in the United States are born exposed to drugs and/or alcohol each year. Fetal Alcohol Syndrome and Effect have been compared to an iceberg – the largest part of the problem is hidden. The problem is so great that I feel it is important to allocate my last chapter to this problem.

It is estimated that over five billion dollars is spent caring for substance-exposed children during their first five years of life. In 1989, the lifetime care of *just one* Fetal Alcohol Syndrome child averaged 1.4 million dollars and the cost increases every year.

Prenatal alcohol exposure is the major cause of preventable mental retardation in this country. Fetal Alcohol Syndrome is recognized by growth retardation, distinctive facial features, and brain damage. It can also cause learning disabilities, hyperactivity, and emotional disorders.

There is a wide range of effects which occur from prenatal exposure to alcohol, and there are differences in how individual children are affected, even within the same family. Some people have only slight problems and live a normal life while others are severely disabled. Several researchers have shown that fraternal twins are usually affected unequally. During my research, I met a pair of identical twins who had different physical anomalies caused by alcohol exposure.

These children, like all children, whether foster, adopted, or birth, are their parent's hopes for the future. But as they grow older, it becomes obvious that there is something seriously wrong. Some parents have had horrendous experiences with their FAS/FAE children. Because these kids are unable to anticipate events in the future, they can't put two things together or wait for a reward. Standard behavior modification doesn't work with them. These kids are difficult to manage and progress is slow. Some are disruptive in school, while others are quiet and withdrawn.

Alcohol injured children may look as though they understand what you're saying. They may smile and agree, then make the same mistake all over again. It appears that they are noncompliant because they can parrot a command that they can't fully understand or follow through with. However they're not being defiant, but have a true disability.

Some are oversensitive to being touched. They experience the slightest touch as painful. A child like this may swing out and hit another person who just brushed against his body or pointed at him. This same behavior is now being reported in cocaine-exposed kids.

The problems found in conjunction with FAS are not a matter of maturation – these children don't outgrow it. One common observation is that adults with FAS don't appear to have a conscience. They don't have any malicious intent, or a criminal mind, but they tend to do whatever pops into their head, and are easily led. They live in the "here and now." They can't predict what the consequences of their actions will be and they don't appear to feel regret about their past conduct.

Although only half the people with FAS have a low enough intelligence to be considered mentally disabled and receive social security benefits, most have decreased intelligence. Fetal alcohol and drug-exposed children learn differently. *However, with help, they are able to learn and adapt to their disabilities.*

Children with FAS need support, love, and patience from their parents to help them compensate for their disabilities, but they often don't get this. Frequent moves, physical and sexual abuse, and poor parenting are common themes in their lives. Substance exposed children overwhelm foster care, social services, and public schools. The problem is everywhere. Like a stone thrown into a pond, their waves radiate out to touch us all.

All children need a stable home to live and grow up in. Although a family setting is the ideal, many children have been so badly hurt by alcohol, drugs, abuse, and constant moves that they're no longer emotionally able to live with any family. We need new programs instead of foster care. *All* children need a permanent living situation, even if this means residential care, group homes, or children's homes for those who are unable to maintain any other placement.

When they become adults, those who are mentally retarded may end up in small group homes, families, or their own apartment rather than the large institutions of the past. Those who are more intelligent, but also disabled, may become street people, just managing to survive day to day. Still others go in and out of psychiatric institutions, or end up in jail.

Years ago, people could stay in a mental "asylum" for life, but this is no longer true. The number of beds in psychiatric hospitals has decreased almost eighty percent over the past twenty years. The advent of psychotropic drugs has helped many mentally ill people leave institutions and live a normal life. But this leaves people with FAS/FAE in limbo.

Even as adults, their judgment impairment puts them at risk for contracting AIDS and they put themselves in dangerous situations. Not only are *they* in danger, society is in danger *from them.* They lie, act impulsively, and show no remorse – they act freely on anything that occurs to them, without considering the consequences. Outrageous behavior is their norm. Until our society begins to protect these "forever children," we can expect a high death rate through accidents, suicides, AIDS, and murders. Those who don't find support in hospitals may end up in jail. These injured individuals need our continued protection.

Fetal Alcohol Syndrome is not only damaging to the children, the alcoholism that causes FAS is often fatal to their mothers. Studies have shown that over half the birthmothers are dead from illness, violence, accidents, or suicide by the time the child is seven years old. *No other birth defect causes this kind of fatality to the parents.* The mother's death is one reason why so many children with FAS enter foster care.

Substance abusing adults and their injured children are a problem our country can no longer afford to ignore. The cost is crippling. Not only in dollars, but in lost potential, suffering, and human life. No one escapes the consequences of substance-damaged children. The evidence is all around us. Our taxes help pay for foster care and other social services they require. We all pay for the institutions, hospitals, and prisons where these children are cared for when they become adults.

Why is it that a country which claims to care for its children doesn't ensure that every baby is born free of alcohol and drug injuries, or help every parent gain the knowledge and resources to properly care for their children?

The answer is not a mystery. We *know* what to do. Hillary Rodham Clinton, our former first lady, was accurate when she said, "It takes a village to raise a child." The most successful programs start with a strong community base. An emphasis on prevention; proactive rather than reactive programs, is essential. The first steps must be prevention, education, and building self-esteem. High school based programs which address drug/alcohol abuse and teen pregnancy are essential to break the cycle of both poverty and child abuse. Offering preventative services to teens and other high-risk parents is crucial. Community based drop-in centers where parents can receive support, parent training, and case management to help them access needed services have proven effective. Visiting nurses, intensive in-home support and training programs have been implemented to assure children remain safe in their homes while parents receive individualized services and training. These programs have proven both successful and cost effective.

However, even with the best services possible, there are going to be some failures. When a home continues to be unsafe, then permanent removal and adoption may be a better answer than long term foster care. The maximum length of foster care has to be limited and a stable placement must be found for all children.

Support services in the future will be new and different from the present care foster care system. We have a long way to go to make appropriate treatment accessible to everyone.

New and comprehensive programs are necessary for both children and their parents. Good programs are not only humane but also cost effective. We can't continue looking towards the same old designs that don't work, but must be open to new programs with proven success. Each successful program gives people control over their lives, helps them earn an education, child-care skills, a good job, and most of all, helps people regain dignity, and a purpose to their lives.

If we are ever to avert the tragedy of foster care – parents losing their children, children being bounced from home to home – this is the direction in which our country must move. The Adoption Assistance and Child Welfare Act, PL96-272, was passed in 1980. This law requires states to provide "reasonable efforts" to prevent removal of children from their homes before the state can receive federal reimbursement for out-of-home care. It also limits the time a child may spend in foster care. The answers exist, and so does the law. Now it is time for us to honestly begin caring for our children. As we enter the twenty-first century, this is the challenge we need to embrace.

PART 2

*"Thou shalt conceive and bear
a son. Therefore beware, and
drink No wine or strong drink..."*

Judges 13:7

FETAL ALCOHOL SYNDROME

HISTORY

The problems related to drug and alcohol use during pregnancy have been recognized as far back as the beginning of recorded history. The Bible warned against it, and so did the ancient Greeks, who passed a law that "prohibited a bride and groom from drinking wine on their wedding night so that defective children would not be conceived." In 1834, a report to the House of Commons in England advised, "Infants born to alcoholic mothers sometimes had a starved, shriveled and imperfect look."

These, and other examples, suggest it has long been known that excessive use of alcohol during pregnancy can damage the fetus. However, in the United States, it was not until 1973 that researchers first described a condition that is now called Fetal Alcohol Syndrome (FAS), or Fetal Alcohol Spectrum Disorder (FASD), which is inclusive of all individuals who were prenatally alcohol exposed.

THE EXTENT OF THE PROBLEM

This birth defect, found only in children whose mothers' drank during their pregnancies, causes facial abnormalities, stunted growth, and brain damage. It runs along a continuum from mild to severe. Children born with less than the full syndrome are considered to have Possible Fetal Alcohol Effect (FAE), or Alcohol-Related Neuro-Developmental Disorders (ARND). Children with FAE appear normal but may have the same neurological disabilities as a child with the full syndrome.

Each year there are 50,000 babies born with alcohol induced birth defects. Researchers suggest FAS/FAE has overtaken Down's syndrome and Spinal Bifida and is now the leading known cause of mental retardation. It is the only one of these three that is totally preventable.

Even though FAS/FAE is the most common cause of developmental disabilities in this country, the majority of doctors, social workers, and other professionals in the field of child services have little knowledge of Fetal Alcohol Syndrome and fail to recognize its symptoms.

This is a national problem that needs addressing – right from the very beginning. In the past, few obstetricians ever asked their patients if they were drinking. For many doctors this remains a sensitive and unmentioned problem. But it needs to be discussed. There are countless women who don't realize that drinking only a few wine coolers or beers on a regular basis might affect their baby. A single binge at a susceptible time in development can also cause damage. Injury to the baby isn't always obvious. Mild learning disabilities or emotional problems may not show up until years later and are unlikely to be associated with those forgotten drinks. The development of facial features is completed early, but the brain continues growing throughout all nine months. Drinking during only the later part of the pregnancy can result in a normal appearing child who might still have severe brain damage. There is no safe time a woman can drink during pregnancy.

HOW MUCH ALCOHOL IS SAFE

No one really knows how much alcohol it takes to cause damage. Approximately one third of pregnant women who drink heavily give birth to children with signs of FAS/FAE. Yet, some children suffer from symptoms of alcohol damage when their mothers drank moderately. It is not a simple one to one equation. Genetics, nutrition, mother's age, gestational age of the fetus, number of previous births, and possibly other unknown factors, all determine when a specific child is at risk.

Since the first American study in 1973 described Fetal Alcohol Syndrome, thousands of research reports have been written on this subject. There are descriptions of babies born with amniotic fluid that smells like alcohol. Babies drink their amniotic fluid; so long after the mother has gone home to sleep off her hangover, the fetus continues ingesting chemicals that are poisonous to its brain and body. But unlike its mother, the baby with its rapidly growing brain may never recover from *its* hangover. Most alcohol-affected children appear normal. Brain damage isn't easily seen, but even when the baby doesn't have any physical features indicating FAS, alcohol exposed infants have disturbed behaviors at birth. They tend to be jittery, stiff, tremulous, restless, and have excessive mouthing movements. They cry or sleep more than normal infants and have fewer quiet-alert periods. When infants are quiet and alert, they are open to learning as well as interacting and bonding with their mothers. A decrease in this state interferes with learning and attachment.

THE SYMPTOMS OF FETAL ALCOHOL SYNDROME

In order to be diagnosed with Fetal Alcohol Syndrome, a child must have growth impairment, distinct facial features and body abnormalities, signs of brain damage, and a maternal history of heavy drinking. A syndrome is a group of features, which together are characteristics of a certain condition. There is no one single feature, which alone can identify the syndrome. All four features must be present before a FAS diagnoses may be made.

The first of these features is growth impairment. At birth FAS children are small (tenth percentile or less) in both weight and length. Infants often have poor sucking ability and are difficult to feed. But even if they get enough calories, they grow poorly and are often considered "failure to thrive." As young children, they are very short and painfully scrawny, often looking as though they have been half starved to death. No matter what they eat they just don't gain the weight they need to grow. To make matters worse, children with FAS are notoriously bad eaters. Many don't seem to care about food and need to be urged to eat. Even as adults they tend to be short, although they eventually catch up in weight. Some surprising studies have now shown that adolescent girls with FAS may tend to become overweight.

The facial features are also distinctive. The majority have short palpebral fissures – the length of the eye is shorter than normal, leaving a wide space between the eyes. Other eye disorders such as crossed, drooped, or jerking eyes are seen. Epicanthic folds, a fold of skin over the inner corner of the eye, is common. Epicanthic folds are also normal features in Asian races and Native Americans, so like the other features of this syndrome, they *do not by themselves* indicate FAS. Other features include a small upturned nose, small head, flattened midface, flattened philtrum (the groove between the nose and lip), thin upper lip, and small jaw. Because the jaw grows with maturity but the head size remains small, adolescents and adults with FAS appear to have larger than normal jaws – although they are actually normal sized. Ears may be placed abnormally low on the head, stick out, be rotated backwards, or oddly shaped. These facial features begin developing in the third week of pregnancy – before most women even know they have conceived.

Prenatal exposure to alcohol can affect other areas of the body. Some of these children have extensive red strawberry birthmarks (hemangiomas) on the back of the neck or other reddened areas on their face or body, but unexposed infants may have this also. These usually fade and disappear in the first year or two of life. Deficiencies in the immune system can lead to chronic colds, poor health, and ear infections. Recent studies have shown that this may be because their bodies have diminished T-cell functions. Heart murmurs are common but are not usually serious. They usually outgrow the heart problems, and if not, it may be correctable though surgery. Cleft palate occurs more often than in the normal population and scoliosis is more likely to develop during adolescence. Other abnormalities include a sunken chest, a lack of formation of the palmar crease – the deep line which runs across the palm up to the second or third finger – joint malformations, crooked fingers or toes, tooth abnormalities, or excessive hair. Although genital malformations may exist, puberty is not delayed.

Brain damage is the most debilitating features of this disorder. Children are usually microcephalic – they have a smaller than normal head indicating a small brain – and have central nervous system (CNS) disorders. This can lead to behavioral problems. Babies with FAS/FAE have trouble adapting to new stimuli. A normal infant may turn or startle to a new sound, but if the sound continues he soon ignores it. However, alcohol exposed children respond abnormally. Some fail to adapt and continue startling with each repeated sound, becoming more and more agitated when they are unable to turn their attention off. Others shut down and fail to respond at all, as though they were deaf and blind. This difficulty remains throughout their life and they continue having trouble attending to what is important and tuning-out what isn't. In childhood, this disability is called attention deficit disorder (ADD), and is frequently found along with hyperactivity.

Temper tantrums, disobedience, impulsiveness, learning problems, seizures, emotional disorders, developmental delays, poor eating and sleeping, are also reported among alcohol exposed children.

Prenatal alcohol exposure affects intelligence and FAS children are often mentally slow or retarded. These babies are delayed walking and developing other motor skills. The muscle tone in infants may be hypotonic (i.e. floppy) and the child may be clumsy. Toilet training is a challenge that may not be mastered until seven or eight years old.

These children are delayed learning to talk and understand speech. They have difficulty following directions and must be given only one command at a time. Like parrots, they are often able to say more than they can understand, giving the impression that they have higher abilities than they really do.

Impaired memory, poor judgment, and the inability to learn from their mistakes are traits that may continue into adulthood. Even those with normal or above normal intelligence have trouble learning the everyday skills they need to survive. More than half continue needing help with basic self care skills and almost none ever learn to balance a checkbook or handle money responsibly.

Research on animals and autopsies on infants who have died of FAS give a clearer reason for these problems. The brains of these children are small and abnormal in structure, as are the brains of animals that were given alcohol prenatally during research studies. When the brain develops in utero, the cells migrate to their correct area and then stop. However, alcohol disrupts this process and the cells continue moving past the point where they should have stopped. This results in a scrambled appearing brain with no clear-cut dark and light areas. The folds and convolutions of the normal brain are decreased so that the alcohol damaged brain is smoother than normal (heterotopic) and the ventricles, or spaces, are enlarged. Unlike the normal brain, there is no clear-cut left and right side.

The last requirement needed to diagnose FAS is the mother's drinking history. Studies show as little as two drinks per day, or five drinks at one time, can cause signs of alcohol damage. Different fetuses have different sensitivity to alcohol exposure. When twins are born, one may have FAS and the other may appear normal.

ADDITIONAL RISK FACTORS

People of European decent seem less affected than races that haven't had a long history of alcohol in their culture. Blacks and Native Americans are especially susceptible, although no population is immune.

The mother's health influences the baby's. A woman who is drinking heavily may not be eating an adequate diet, and this can lead to a smaller baby. But malnutrition does not cause FAS. Use of street drugs or cigarettes can also lead to a smaller, less healthy baby. The mother's age seems to make a difference and later children in the family are at greater risk of being affected. When a woman has already had one FAS/FAE child, the risk of later children being impaired is as high as 75 percent if she continues drinking.

There is no cure for Fetal Alcohol Syndrome/Effect, only prevention. There is no placental barrier – the fetus has an alcohol level equal to its mother.

This disorder is completely preventable. If all pregnant women refrained from drinking, there would never be another baby born with FAS.

*American feelings about drugs fluctuate.
During the past 200 years we have
twice embraced, and then rejected drug usage.*

CRACK COCAINE AND OTHER DRUGS

HISTORY

There is evidence of drug use nearly as far back as the beginning of humanity. There are presently non-technical cultures in South America which grow coca and "chew" the leaves. Actually, a wad of coca leaves is put in between the cheek and gums and sucked – never chewed. An alkaline powder such as bicarbonate or wood ash is added to the wad to increase salivation and release of alkaloids. The drug in the leaves of these unprocessed plants is a dilute form of cocaine.

The real problems didn't appear until new knowledge of organic chemistry in the 1800's allowed drugs to be processed and concentrated.

Psychoactive drugs were legal in the United States in the 1800's. Cough medicines contained mixtures of opium, morphine, codeine, or heroin. A few grains of cocaine added to alcohol was a popular drink at this time. Coca-Cola was introduced in 1886 as an alternative to the alcoholic beverage, although it still contained cocaine. Parker-Davis sold cocaine in fifteen different forms including cigarettes, snuff, and injection.

However, as awareness about the danger of these drugs became known, they became less popular. In 1900, Coca-cola took the cocaine out of its formula. In January 1920, the temperance law was passed which prohibited alcohol. It was not until a whole generation later in the 1960's and 70's that drugs again became popular. Now, as a new generation is learning the damaging effects, history is repeating itself and drug use is again becoming discredited.

COCAINE

In recent years, newer and more addictive drugs have become available. Crack, a concentrated form of cocaine, is a powerful stimulant. It reaches the brain within seconds and gives a tremendous high. It also causes blood vessels in the body to constrict. This causes the heart rate and blood pressure to go up and can result in a heart attack or stroke – even in a healthy adult. The intense high doesn't last long and is followed by severe depression and a need for more drugs. This is what makes crack so addictive.

Different drugs, dosage, and purity of drugs, trimester of pregnancy, diet, lifestyle, lack of prenatal care, and individual genetic differences all muddle the picture of how each drug affects the fetus. The mother's cocaine high ends quickly and is followed by severe depression. To help ease out of this depression, she uses other drugs – usually tobacco, marijuana, and alcohol. Yes, alcohol. It's legal, relatively cheap, and socially acceptable. It's even advertised. No wonder many cocaine-exposed babies appear to have Fetal Alcohol Syndrome. "Cocaine babies" are usually polydrug babies in that they have been exposed to many different substances. To further confuse things, mothers do not readily admit to drug use and tests only pick up substances taken within the past few days. All these factors make research difficult.

When a pregnant woman uses cocaine, the drug goes though the umbilical cord and the baby gets high as quickly as the mother. Residuals of cocaine use remain in the adult body for one or two days. Cocaine, being fat soluble, mixes with the mother's blood and crosses the placenta into the fetus. The fetus breaks the cocaine down into two other chemicals: benzoylecgonine and norcocaine. Benzoylecgonine remains mixed with the blood and is quickly returned to the mother. However, norcocaine becomes a problem because it is water soluble, mixes with the fetus's urine, and is passed into the amniotic fluid where the mother's body can't remove it. The baby swallows the amniotic fluid and continues getting high for four to five more days as it keeps ingesting the drug. Its blood pressure and heartbeat are high and the baby is jittery. According to Dr Ira Chasnoff, director of the National Association of Perinatal Addiction Research and Education, when you buzz a sound to a normal fetus, it moves around a bit and then calms down. A baby exposed to cocaine can't calm itself down. Its heart rate stays up for hours.

Cocaine causes blood vessels to constrict, which raises the heart rate, and also causes uterine contractions. In early pregnancy, it can cause spontaneous abortion (miscarriages) and is sometimes used to end an unwanted pregnancy. When used later in pregnancy, it can cause premature labor. One third of cocaine-exposed infants are born prematurely. Even if the mother only used cocaine during her first trimester, there is an increased chance that the placenta will separate from the wall of the uterus too soon, resulting in bleeding, lack of oxygen, and possibly death to the fetus and mother.

Premature birth occurs in one third of these pregnancies. Premature infants require weeks or moths of intensive care. Hospital costs for these babies are approximately $1,500 to $2,000 *per day*. An infant born at 32 weeks gestation (eight weeks premature) may need two months of intensive care at a cost of over $100,000. The earlier an infant is born, the more complicated and expensive care he requires. These babies are not only born early, many are smaller than would be expected for their gestational age.

Unless they also have Fetal Alcohol Syndrome, *most* cocaine-exposed infants appear normal and do not have obvious birth defects. However, the rate of birth defects is higher among cocaine-exposed infants than in unexposed children. When blood vessels contract because of cocaine, blood flow to the fetus is reduced. This can cause the baby to have brain damage, a heart attack, or a stroke during its birth.

Lack of blood flow during early development is also suspected in causing abnormalities of the urinary tract and genital areas. A condition called prune-belly, in which abnormalities of the abdominal muscles and bladder give the stomach a wrinkled, prune-like appearance, occurs more often in cocaine exposed infants. Heart malformations, skull defects and intestinal blockages also seem to occur more frequently in these children than in the general population.

Except when there was alcohol involved, mental retardation isn't a factor for most drug-exposed children. Brain damage in cocaine-exposed children is subtler. Studies show some of these children have small heads and are at risk for long-term developmental problems. Brain growth is measured through head circumference. Electroencephalograms, or EEGs, show that one third of these babies have abnormalities in their brains. There abnormal behavior also indicates brain damage.

Cocaine exposed babies don't go through drug withdrawal the way those exposed to alcohol or heroin do. However, they often have tremors that last for months. These seem related to brain dysfunction rather than withdrawal. Many of these children are hypertonic: they have stiff muscle tone, which interferes with movement. Seizures are also common. Some studies have shown an increased rate of Sudden Infant Death Syndrome (SIDS), but the evidence is inconclusive. Some studies have shown that the SIDS rate is higher among infants in the care of their natural mothers than in foster or adoptive homes.

Many drug-exposed infants avoid eye contact, seem sleepy and withdrawn, or go to the other extreme and cry excessively. These behaviors are attempts to shut off the outside world. They need a calm, quiet environment with as little stimulation as possible. There is a special rocking technique which seems to help relax them: the baby is held away from the adult's body and rocked in an up and down, rather than sideways, motion.

It is hard for healthy adults to care for a fussy or unresponsive infant and it's even worse for mothers who are recovering from a cocaine habit or are still using. They are not ready to parent such difficult infants and they need a great deal of support, something they probably don't have. It's easy to see how the combination of an infant who sleeps all day, or screams constantly, and an impaired mother without adequate support, can result in serious problems such as failure to thrive or even the infant's death.

Learning, attention problems, and hyperactivity have been reported in cocaine-exposed preschoolers. They are slow learning to talk and understand speech, have temper tantrums, and are constantly moving from one activity to another. They may use a doll or toy to throw or hit another child rather than for imaginary play. They seem overloaded by their environment, as though they were wired for 110 volts in a 220-volt world. A normal environment is just too much for them to handle all at once.

Not all cocaine-exposed children are like this. Some are withdrawn, or just slow learners. Others appear to outgrow their early problems, and seem all right.

Environment plays an important role in how well these children function. Even a child without the complicating factors of prenatal drug and alcohol exposure wouldn't do well in a chaotic home environment with drug abusing parents or constantly being bounced from foster home to foster home.

OPIATES: HEROIN AND METHADONE

Infants exposed to opiates such as heroin and methadone go though severe drug withdrawal at birth. They suffer from shaking, yawning, irritability, poor sucking, failure to gain weight, diarrhea, severe tremors, and possible death. These symptoms tend to disappear within the first two months, although irritability may continue for the first year or longer. *Methadone, which is given to help women stay off heroin, is just as bad, or worse, for the infant.*

These drugs are not a cause of birth defects and they do not cause mental retardation or decreased intelligence.

Opiate exposed infants may be small at birth; however, given a good environment, they soon catch up. If they live in a stable household with capable parents they do well. Children whose parents abuse drugs tend to have problems whether or not they were exposed prenatally.

MARAJUANA

At one time marijuana was suspected of causing abnormal facial features similar to Fetal Alcohol Syndrome. This has now been disproved. This confusion came about because many women who use marijuana also drink. Like most of the drugs being discussed here, marijuana does not cause any obvious birth defects. Infants of marijuana users tend to be small, although this could be a reflection of the mothers' diet rather than drug use. Some studies show that marijuana interacts with alcohol, causing more problems than if either one was used alone. Newborn babies of heavy marijuana users have more tremors and startle easier than unexposed infants. Although there are some studies that suggest that intelligence of these children may be slightly decreased, the long-term effects are not known and these children appear normal.

TOBACCO

Cigarette smoke contains over 2000 different substances including such deadly compounds as carbon monoxide and cyanide. Nicotine, a chemical that causes addiction, crosses the placenta. Nicotine causes the fetuses' blood vessels to contract and reduces its oxygen.

Although there are no known birth defects connected to cigarette smoking, smoker's babies are slightly smaller than are the babies of non-smokers. The infants of smokers are at a greater risk of having breathing related illnesses such as asthma, bronchitis, or pneumonia, and of dying from sudden infant death syndrome.

Skippy King, a licensed midwife who delivered babies at home for many years, refused to accept clients who smoked.

"The placenta of a smoker smells like a dirty ashtray," she explained. "A smoker wouldn't notice but I have a sensitive nose. The odor is very potent and vile to me. A smoker's placenta is gray. Normally it would be royal red like fresh beef liver. It is not as healthy and not able to nourish the baby as long. Smokers' babies are small for their due date but not usually premature.

"The labors are longer and harder. I think it's because the mothers have less air and are not able to handle the contractions as well. The babies don't catch on as fast and don't breathe as easily. They need a puff of air to get started.

"I don't think a smoker should have a home birth because they need oxygen. They have to be in a hospital. I don't like to take those births, there always seems to be some problems."

OTHER DRUGS

This list is not complete, many new "designer-drugs" have become available in the past decade. All drugs, legal or illegal, must be used with care during pregnancy. Any treatment or medication prescribed by a doctor, which causes birth defects is called an Iatrogen. During the 1950s and early '60s, Thalidomide was given to pregnant women in Germany. As a result, babies were born without arms or legs and were frequently deaf. In the United States, an estrogen hormone, diethylstilbestrol (DES), given to pregnant women, was found to cause cervical cancer or testicular abnormalities when the exposed babies became adults. Bendectin, an anti-nausea drug, was later proved to cause cleft palate and neural tube defects in babies. Thalidomide was never widely used in the United States, and both DES and Bendectin have been taken off the market. Other drugs such as Streptomycin can cause deafness and Retin A, given for acne, causes facial defects, as do many of the anticonvulsant drugs such as Dilantin and Depakane. Dilantin can cause Fetal Hydantoin (Meadow's) Syndrome, a condition that looks very much like Fetal Alcohol Syndrome. Although the physical effects of these drugs are well documented, their effects on immunity and behavior are still being studied.

AIDS

Acquired Immune Deficiency Syndrome (AIDS) is a serious problem among drug abusing women. They catch the disease from infected needles or though sexual contact. Antibodies pass from the mother to the infant, so a baby can test positive for HIV (Human Immunodeficiency Virus) up to fifteen months after birth, even if he doesn't have the virus or disease himself. Thus, tests on an infant show only that the mother has been exposed to the HIV virus, not whether the child will develop the disease. One fourth of the cocaine-exposed infants have been exposed to HIV and half of these will develop the disease. Presently there is not yet a cure for AIDS, and although medications can extend an individuals life for many years, the disease eventually leads to death.

Bibliography

Chasnoff, I. J. (Ed.)., (1989). *Drugs, alcohol, pregnancy and parenting.* Kluwer Academic Publishers.

Doris, M., (1989). *The broken cord.* New York:Harper Perennial.

Magid, K., & McKelvey, C.A., (1988). *High risk: children without a conscience* New York:Bantam Books

Streissguth, A. P., LaDue, R A., & Randels, S.P., (1988). *A manual on adolescents and adults with special reference to American Indians.* Us Department of Health and Human services.

Kleinfeld, J. & Wescott,S., (1993). *Fantastic Antone succeeds! experiences in educating children with fetal alcohol syndrome.* University of Alaska Press.

BONDING, ATTACHMENT, AND CHILD DEVELOPMENT

Adams, E.J., (1991). *Loss of innocence: a try story of juvenile murder.* New York:Avon Books.

Beck, J.W., (1986). *How to raise a brighter child: the case for early learning.* New York:Simon & Schuster.

Beckwith, L., Rodning, C,. & Cohen, S., (1992). Preterm children at early adolescence and continuity and discontinuity in maternal responsiveness from infancy. *Child Development,* 63(5):1198-1208.

Brazelton, B. T., (1984). *To listen to a child.* New York:Addison-Wesley Publishing Co.

Collins, M., & Tamarkin, C., (1990). *Marva Collins way: returning to excellence in education.* New York:Putman Publishing.

Doman, G., (1990). *What to do about your brain-injured child.* Philadelphia, P.A.:The Better Baby Press.

Fahlberg, S., (1979). *Attachment and Separation.* Michigan Department of Social Services.

Isabella, R.A., (1993). Origins of attachment: maternal interactive behavior across the first year. *Child Development,* 64(2):605-621

Jewett, C.L., (1978). *Adopting the older child.* The Harvard Common Press.

Kreisman, J.J., & Straus, H., (1989). *I hate you: don't leave me.* Price Stern Sloan, Inc.

Levy, J., (1973). *The baby exercise book.* New York: Random House.

Lewis, D., (1981). *How to be a gifted parent: realize your child's full potential.* New York: Norton.

Lyons R.K., Alpern, L., & Tepacholi, B., (1993). Disorganized infant attachment classification and maternal psychosocial problems as predictors of hostile-aggressive behavior in the preschool classroom. *Child Development.* 64(2):572-585

Magid, K., & McKelvey, C.A., (1988). *High risk: children without a conscience* New York:Bantam Books

Montagu, A., (1971). *Touching: the human significance of the skin.* Perennial Library, New York:Harper & Row.

Paluszny, M.J., (1979). *Autism.* Syracuse University Press.

Samenow, S.E., (1989). *Before it's too late.* New York:Times books.

Samenow, S.E., (1984). *Inside the Criminal Mind.* New York: Crown Business.

FOSTER CARE, SOCIAL SERVICES, AND ALTERNATIVE PROGRAMS

Allen, M., (1991). Crafting a federal legislative framework for child welfare reform. *American Journal of Orthopsychiatry.* 61(4):610-623

Allen, M., (1993). Federal legislative update. *Frontlineviews.* 3:8-9.

Armstrong, L., (1989). *Solomon says: a speakout on foster care.* New York: Simon & Schuster.

Barthel, J., (1992). *For children's sake: the promise of family preservation.* Edna McConnell Clark Foundation.

Bath, H., Haapala, D.A., (1993). Intensive family preservation services with abused and neglected children: an examination of group differences. *Child Abuse and Neglect.* 17(2):213-225.

Bryant, J., (1988). A public-private partnership builds support for family preservation services. *Children Today.* 17(1):25-27.

Campinha-Bacote, J., & Bragg, E.J., (1993). Chemical assessment in maternity care. *The American Journal of Maternal/Child Nursing.* 18(1):24-28.

Carroll, K., Rounsaville, B., & Bryant, K., (1993), Alcoholism in treatment-seeking cocaine abusers:clinical and prognostic significance. *Journal of Studies on Alcohol.* 54(2):199-208.

Chasnoff, I.J., (1989). Drug use and women: establishing a standard of care. *Annals of the New York Academy of Sciences.* 562:208-210.

Chisum, G., (1990). Nursing interventions with the antepartum substance abuser. *The Journal of Perinatal and Neonatal Nursing.* 3(4):26-33

Department of Social Services (undated)., *Family first guidelines, children's protective services.* Lansing, Michigan.

Department of Social Services (undated)., *Family first guidelines, foster care: reunification.* Lansing, Michigan.

Doelling, J.L., & Johnson, J.H., (1990). Predicting success in foster placement: the contribution of parent-child temperament characteristics. *American Journal of Orthopsychiatry*. 60(4):585-593.

Donnelly, A. C., (1992). Healthy family American. *Children Today*. 21(2):12-13.

Fagin, A., & Reid, A., (1991). Moms in jail. *Children Today*. 20(1):12-13.

Fein, E., (1991). The elusive search for certainty in child welfare: introduction. *American Journal of Orthopsychiatry*. 61(4):576-577.

Fein, E., (1991). Issues in foster family care: where do we stand? *American Journal of Orthopsychiatry*. 61(4):578-583.

Fontana, V.J. & Moolman, V., (1991). *Save the family, save the child: what we can do to help children at risk*. New York: Dutton.

Hwnwaon, L., (1992). The secretary's initiative on child abuse and neglect. *Children Today*. 21(2):4-7.

Hulsey, T.C., & White, R., (1989) Family characteristics and measures of behavior in foster and non foster children. *American Journal of Orthopsychiatry*. 59(4):502-509.

Jiordano, M.J., (1991) Back to basics approach to working with substance-affected families. *Frontlineviews*.

Luginbill, M., & Spiegler, A., (1989) Specialized foster family care. *Children Today*. 61(4):606-609.

Marion, R., (1990). *The boy who felt no pain*. New York, Addison-Wesley Publishing Co.

McCuen, G.E., (1991). *Born hooked: poisoned in the womb*. Publications Inc.

Newton, R.W., Hunt, L.P., (1984). Psychosocial stress in pregnancy and it's relationship to low birth weight. *British Medical Journal*. 288:1191-1194

Rist, M.C., (1990). The shadow children. *The American School Board Journal.* 14-19.

Shaywitz, B.A., Cohen, D.J., & Shaywitz, S., (1979). New diagnostic terminology for minimal
brain dysfunction. *The Journal of Pediatrics.* 95:734-736.

Merson, M.J., (1992). AIDS: the world situation. *Journal of Public Health Policy.* 13(1):18-26

Michigan Department of Social Services., (1990) *Families first of Michigan.* Lansing Michigan.

Myers, M. G., (1989). Families of welfare: foster children with special needs. *Children Today.*
18(4):6-9.

Neergaard, J., (1990). A proposal for a foster grandmother intervention program to prevent child
Abuse. *Public Health Reports.* 105(1):89-93.

Phelps, D., (1989). Foster home recruitment and retention: a success story. *Children Today.*
18(2):7-9.

Pinderhughes, E.E., (1991). The delivery of child welfare services to African American clients.
American Journal of Orthopsychiatry. 61 (4):599-605.

Public Law 96-272, The adoption assistance and child welfare act of 1980. 96th Congress, 94.
Stat. 500-535, Vol. 94, Pt. 1.

Paurcell, B., (1993). Home ties: preventing placement across systems. *Frontlineviews.* 3:4-7

Rhodes, A., (1992) Criminal penalties for maternal substance abuse. *The American Journal of Maternal/child nursing.* 17(1):11.

Roberts, R. N., McLaughlin, G.B., & Mulvey, L., (1991). Family support in the home: lessons
from pioneer programs. *Children Today.* 20(1):14-17.

Robison, S., & Binder, H., (1993), Building bridges for families. *Frontlineviews.* 3:1-3.

Sokol, R.J., Miller, S.I., & Martier, S., (1981). Preventing fetal alcohol effects: a practical guide for OB/Gyn physicians and nurses. *National Institute on Alcohol Abuse and Alcoholism,* Rockville, M.D.

Sylvia, A., (1991). *When the bough breaks: the cost of neglecting our children.* New York:Hewlett Basic Books.

Velsor-Friedrich, B., (1992). Poverty: it's effects on children and their families. *Journal of Pediatric Nursing: Nursing Care of Children ad Families.* 7(6):412-413.

Widom, C.S., (1991)., (The role of placement experiences in mediating the criminal consequences of early childhood victimization. *The American Journal of Orthopsychiatry.* 61(2):195-209.

Wolfner, G.D., & Gelles, R.J., (1993). A profile of violence toward children: a national study. *Child Abuse and Neglect.*

Wolock, I., & Horowitz, B., (1984). Child Maltreatment as a social problem: the neglect of neglect. *The American Journal of Orthopsychiatry.* 54(4):530-543.

CRACK COCAINE AND OTHER DRUGS

Alkins, W.T., (1989). *Cocaine: the drug of choice.* Drugs, Alcohol, Pregnancy and Parenting (Ed.), Chasnoff, I.J. Kluwer Academic Publishers.

Bandstra, E., (1992). *Medical consequences of in-utero cocaine exposure.* Substance abuse, pregnancy and childrearing: children deserve better. Presentation at the fifth annual PAR conference.

Barr, M., Pozanski. A.K., & Schmickel, R.D. (1974). Digital hypoplasia and anticonvulsants during gestation, a terratogenic syndrome. *Jornal of Pediatrics.* 84:254-256.

Bozarth, M.A., & Wise, R.A., (1985). Toxicity associated with long-term intravenous heroin and cocaine self-administration in the rat. *Journal of the American Medical Association.* 154:81-83.

Brixey, S.N. Gallagher,B.J., McFalls, J.A., & Parmeless, L.F., (1993). Gestational and neonatal factors in the etiology of schizophrenia. *Journal of Clinical Psychology.* 41(3):447-456

Burns, W.J., & Burns, K. A., (1989). *Parenting dysfunction in chemically dependent women.* Drugs, Alcohol, Pregnancy and Parenting (Ed.), Chasnoff, I.J. Kluwer Academic Publishers.

Chadwick, E.G. (1989). *AIDS in pregnancy and the newborn.* Drugs, Alcohol, Pregnancy and Parenting (Ed.), Chasnoff, I.J. Kluwer Academic Publishers.

Chasnoff, I. J., (1989). *Cocaine: effects of the pregnancy and the neonate.* Drugs, Alcohol, Pregnancy and Parenting (Ed.), Chasnoff, I.J. Kluwer Academic Publishers.
Chasnoff, I.J., (1988) *Drugs, alcohol and parenting.* Presentation at the third annual meeting of NAPAR, New York.

Chasnoff, I. J., (1989). *The interfaces of Perinatal addiction. .* Drugs, Alcohol, Pregnancy and Parenting (Ed.), Chasnoff, I.J. Kluwer Academic Publishers.

Cook, P.S., Petersen, R.C., & Moore D.T., (1990). *Alcohol, tobacco, and other drugs may harm the unborn.* DHHS Publication No. (ADFM) 90-1711.

Daghestani, A.N., (1989). *Psychosocial characteristics of pregnant women addicts in treatment.* Drugs, Alcohol, Pregnancy and Parenting (Ed.), Chasnoff, I.J. Kluwer Academic Publishers.

Dalterio, S. L., (1984). Marijuana and the unborn. *Listen, a Journal of Better Living.*

Ellis, J.E., Byrd, L.D., & Sexson, W.R., (1993). In utero exposure to cocaine: a review *Southern Medical Journal.* 86(7):725-731.

Frazer T,M., Davis, G.H., Goldstein, H., & Goldberg, I.D., (1961). Cigarette smoking and prematurity:a prospective study. *American Journal of Obstetrics and Gynecology.* 81:988-996.

Finnegan, L,. (1972). Clinical effects of pharmacological agents on pregnancy, the fetus, and the neonate. *Annals of the New York Academy of Science.* 197:167-169.

Finnegan, L.P., (1989). *Drug addiction and pregnancy: the newborn.* . Drugs, Alcohol, Pregnancy and Parenting (Ed.), Chasnoff, I.J. Kluwer Academic Publishers.

Fried, P.A., (1993). Prenatal exposure to tobacco and marijuana: effects during pregnancy, infancy, and early childhood. *Clinical Obstetrics & Gynecology.* 36(2):319-337.

Fried, P.A., & Oxorn, H., (1980). *Smoking for two: cigarettes and pregnancy.* The Free Press.

Gruffith, D.R., (1989). The effects of Perinatal cocaine exposure on infant neurobehavior and early maternal-infant interactions. Drugs, Alcohol, Pregnancy and Parenting (Ed.), Chasnoff, I.J. Kluwer Academic Publishers.

Hanson, J.W., & Smith, D.W., (1975). The fetal hydantoin syndrome. *Journal of Pediatrics.* 87:285-290.

Hardy, J.B., & Mellitis, E.D., (1972). Does maternal smoking have a long-term effect on the child? *Lancet.* 2:1332-1336.

Harpring, Jayme (ed)., (undated). *Cocaine babies: Florida's substance-exposed youth.* Office of Policy Research and Improvement.

Herriot, A., Billewicz, W.Z., & Hytten, F.E., (1962). Cigarette smoking in pregnancy. *Lancet* 1:771-773.
Hingson, R,. Alpert, J,. Day, N., Dooking, E., Kayne, H., Morlock, S., Oppenheimer, E., & Zuckerman, B. (1982). Effects on maternal drinking and marijuana use on fetal growth and development. *Pediatrics.* 70:539-545.

Illinois Department of Children and Family Services., (1988). *Blizzard in the womb.* Vol.8, no.1.

Kandall, S.R., Gaines, J., Habel, L., Davidson, G., & Jessop, D., (1993). Relationship of maternal substance abuse to subsequent sudden infant death syndrome in offspring. *Journal of Pediatrics.* 123(1):120-126.

Kosofsky, B.E., (1991). The effects of cocaine on developing human brain. *Methodological Issues in Controlled Studies on Effects of Prenatal Exposure to Drug Abuse.* Research Monograph 114.

Kronsstadt, D., (1991). *Complex developmental issues of prenatal drug exposure.* The Future of Children, The David and Lucille Packard Foundation, Vol. 1. No. 1.

Lewis,K., (1992). *Neurobehavioral characteristics of infants prenatally drug exposed.* Substance Abuse, Pregnancy and Childrearing:"Children Deserve Better." Presentation at the fifth annual PAR conference.

Lifschitz, M.H., (1992). *Narcotic abuse in pregnancy, long term effects of the child.* . Substance Abuse, Pregnancy and Childrearing:"Children Deserve Better." Presentation at the fifth annual PAR conference.

Lutiger, B., Graham, K., Einarson, T.R., & Koren, G. (1986). Relationship between gestational cocaine use and pregnancy outcome: a meta-analysis. *Teratology.* 44(4):405-414.

Madden, J., Payne, T., & Miller, S., (1986). Maternal cocaine abuse and effect on the newborn. *Pediatrics.* 77(2):209-210.

March of Dimes Birth Defects Foundation., (1991). *Cocaine use during pregnancy.* Public Health information sheet update.

Shepard, T.H., (1989). *Catalog of teratogenic agents.* The John Hopkins University Press.

Szetim H.H., (1983). Effects of narcotic drugs on fetal behavioral activity: acute methadone exposure. *American Journal of Obstetrics and Gynecology.* 146:211-216.

Tikkanen, E.Z., Beeghly, M., Fetters, L., & Weinberg, K.M., (1991). New methodologies for evaluating residual brain damage in infants exposed to drug abuse: objective methods for describing movements, facial expressions, and communicative behaviors. *Methodological*

Issues in Controlled Studies on Effects of Prenatal Exposure to Drug Abuse. Research Monograph 114.

Weston, D.R., Ivins, B., Zuckerman, B., Jones, C., & Lopez, R., (1989). Drug exposed babies:research and clinic issues. *Zero to Three, National Center for Clinical Infant Programs.* Vol. IX, No. 5.

Wilcox A.J. (1993). Birth weight and Perinatal morality: the effect of maternal smoking. *American Journal of Epidemiology.* 137(10):1098-1104

Zelson, C., Rubio, E., & Wasserman, E., (1971). Neonatal narcotic addiction: ten year observation. *Pediatrics.* 48:178-189.

Zuckerman, B., (1989). *Drug-exposed infants: understanding the medical risk.* The Future of Children, The David and Lucille Packard Foundation, Vol. 1. No. 1.

Zuckerman, B., (1989). *Marijuana and cigarette smoking during pregnancy: neonatal effects.*
Drugs, Alcohol, Pregnancy and Parenting (Ed.), Chasnoff, I.J. Kluwer Academic Publishers.

FETAL ALCOHOL SYNDROME

Abel, E.L., (1983). *Fetal alcohol syndrome and fetal alcohol effects.* New York: Plenum Press.

Abel, E.L. (1988) . Fetal alcohol syndrome in families. *Neurotoxicology and Teratology.* 10(1):1-2.

Abel, E.L. (1989). Paternal behavioral mutagenesis. *Neurotoxicology.* 10(3):335-345.

Abel, E.L., & Sokol, R.J., (1986). Fetal alcohol syndrome is now the leading cause of mental retardation. *Lancet.* 2:1222.

Abel, E.L., & Sokol, R.J., (1987). Incidence of fetal alcohol syndrome and economic impact of FAS-related anomalies. *Drug Alcohol Dependency.* 19:51-70.

Abel, E.L., & Sokol, R.J., (1991). A revised estimate of the economic impact of fetal alcohol syndrome. *Recent Developments in Alcoholism.* 9:117-125.

Becker, M., Warr-Leeper, G.A., & Leeper, H.A., (1980). Fetal alcohol syndrome: a description of oral motor, articulatory, short-term memory, grammatical, and semantic abilities. *Journal of Communicative Disorders.* 23(2):97-124.

Bonthius, D.J., & West, J.R., (1988). Binge alcohol consumption produces more microencephaly with less with less alcohol in neonatal rats. *Teratology.* 37:447.

Bray, D.L., & Anderson, P.D., (1989). Appraisal of the epidemiology of fetal alcohol syndrome among Canadian Native peoples. *Canadian Journal of Public Health.* 80(1):42-45.

Burgess, D.M., & Streissguth, A.P., (1990). Educating students with fetal alcohol syndrome or fetal alcohol effects. *Pennsylvania Reporter.* Vol. 22, No. 1.

Carney, L.J,. & Chermak,G.D., (1991) Performance of American Indian children with fetal alcohol syndrome on the test of language development. *Journal of Communicative Disorders.* 24(2):25-29

Caruso, K,. & ten Bensel, R., (1993). Fetal alcohol syndrome and fetal alcohol effects. *Minnesota Medicine.* 76(4):25-29.

Cahn, T., Bowell, R., O'Keefe, M., & Lanigan, B., (1991). Icular magnifications in fetal alcohol syndrome. *British Journal of Ophthalmology.* 75(9):534-526.

Chernick,V., Childiaeva, R., & Ioffe, S., (1983). Effects of maternal alcohol intake and smoking on neonatal electrocephalogram and anthropolmetric measurements. *American Journal of Obstetrics and Gynecology.* 146:41-47.

Chernoff, G.F. (1977). The fetal alcohol syndrome in mice: an animal model. *Teratology.* 15:223-230

Christiffel, K.K., & Salafsky, Ira., (1975). Fetal alcohol syndrome in dizygotic twins. *The Journal of Pediatrics.* 87:963-967.

Church, M.W., & Gerkin, K.P. (1988). Hearing disorders in children with fetal alcohol syndrome:findings from case reports. *Pediatrics.* 82(2):147-154.

Clarren, S.K., (1981). Recognition for fetal alcohol syndrome. *Journal of the American Medical Association.* 245(23):2436-2439.

Clarren, S.K. Bowden, D.M., & Ashley, S., (1985). The brain in the fetal alcohol syndrome. *Alcohol Health and Research World.* 10(1):20.

Clarren, S.K., Ellsworth, C., Alvord, S., Sumi, M., Streissguth, A.P., & Smith, D.W. (1978). Brain malformations related to prenatal exposure to ethanol. *Journal of Pediatrics.* 92:64-67.

Clarren, S.K., & Smith, D.W., (1978). The fetal alcohol syndrome. *New England Journal of Medicine.* 289(19):1063-1067.

Coles, C.D., Smith, I.E., Fernhoff, P.M., & Falek, A., (1984). Neonatal ethanol withdrawal: characteristics in clinically normal, nondysmorphic neonates. *Journal of Pediatrics.* 105:445-451.

Cornelius, M.D., Day, N.L.,Cornelius, J.R., Taylor, P.M., & Richardson, G.A., (1993). Drinking patterns and correlates of drinking among pregnant teenagers. *Alcoholism.* 17(2):290-294.

Dawson, D.A., (1992). The effect of parental alcohol dependence on perceived children's behavior. *Journal of Substance Abuse.* 4(4):329-340.

Day, N.L., & Richardson, G.A., (1991). Prenatal alcohol exposure: a continuum of effects. *Seminars in perinatology.* 15(4):271-279.

Dedam, R., McFarlane C., & Hennessy, K., (1993). A dangerous lack of understanding. *Canadian Nurse.* 89(6):29-31.

DeVries, J., (1992). The FAS Adolescent Task Force: an army of velveteen rabbits. *Iceberg.* Vol.2, No.2.

Dorris, M., (1989) *The broken cord.* New York: Harper and Row Publishers Inc.

Ewing, D.A. (1984). Detecting alcoholism: the Cage questionnaire. *Journal of the American Medical Association.* 252:1905-1907.

Ferrier, P.E., Nicod, I.., & Ferrier, S., (1973). Fetal alcohol syndrome. *Lancet.* 2:1496.

Fine, E.W., Yudia, L.W., Holms, J., & Heinemann, S., (1976). Behavioral disorders in children with parental alcoholism. *Annals of the New York Academy of Sciences.* 273:507-517.

Foster, U.G., & Baird, P.A., (1992). Congenital defects of the limbs and alcohol exposure in pregnancy: data from a populatin based study. *American Journal of Medical Genetics.* 44(6): 782-785.

Gentry, David., & Middaugh, Lawrence, D., (1988). Prenatal ethanol weakens the efficacy of reinforcers for adult mice. *Teratology.* 37:135-144.

Gir, A.V., Aksharanugraha, K., & Harris, E.F., (1989). A cephalometric assessement of children with fetal alcohol syndrome. *American Journal of Orthodontics and Dentofacial Orthopedics.* 95(4):319-326.

Giunta, C.T., & Streissguth, A.P., (1988). Patients with fetal alcohol syndrome and their caretakers. *Social Casework: The Journal of Contemporary Social Work.* 453-459. Sept.

Glttesfeld, Z., & Abel, E.L., (1991). Maternal and paternal alcohol use: effects on the immune system of the offspring. *Life Sciences.* 48(1):1-8.

Hanson, J.W., Jones, K.L., & Smith, D.L., (1976). Fetal alcohol experience with 41 patients. *Journal of the American Medical Association.* 235:1458-1460.

Hanson, J.W., Streissguth, A.P., & Smith D.L., (1978). The effects of moderate alcohol consumption during pregnancy on fetal growth and morphogenesis. *The Journal of Pediatrics.* 92:457-460.

Hill, R.M., Hegemier,S., & Tennyson, L.M., (1989). The fetal alcohol syndrome: a multihandicapped child. *Neurotoxicology.* 10(3):585-595.

Huffine, C., (1992). A psychiatrist's experience with FAS/FAE. *Iceberg.* Vol. 2, No.4.

Ioffe, S., & Chernick, V., (1988). Development of the EEG between 30 and 40 weeks gestation in normal and alcohol-exposed infants. *Developmental Medicine and Child Neurology.* 30(6):797-807.

Jackson, I.T., & Hussain, K., (1990). Crainiofacial and oral manifestations of fetal alcohol syndrome. *Plastic and Reconstructive Surgery.* 85(4):505:512.

Jones, K.L., Smith, D.W., Streissguth, A.P., & Myrianthopoulos, N.C., (1974). Outcome in offspring of chronic alcoholic women. *Lancet.* 1:1076-1078.

Jones, K.L., & Smith, D.W., (1975). The fetal alcohol syndrome. *Teratology.* 12:1-10.

Jones, K.L. & Smith, D.W., (1973). The recognition of the fetal alcohol syndrome in early infancy. *Lancet.* 2:999-1001.

Jones, K.L. & Smith, D.W., & Hanson, J.W., (1976). The fetal alcohol syndrome: clinical delineation. *Annals of the New York Academy of Sciences.* 273:130-137.

Kennedy, L.A., (1984). The pathogenesis of brain abnormalities in the fetal alcohol syndrome: an integrating hypothesis. *Teratology.* 29:363-368.

LaDue, R., (1992). *Substance abuse, pregnancy and childrearing: "Children Deserve Better."* Operation PAR, fifth annual conference. Clearwater, Florida.

Marcus, J.C., (1987). Neurological findings in the fetal alcohol syndrome. *Neuropediatrics.* 18:158-160.

May, P.A., & Hymbaugh, K.J., (1989). A Macro-level fetal alcohol syndrome prevention program for Native Americans and Alaska

Natives: description and evaluation. *Journal of Studies on Alcohol.* 50(6): 508-518.

Miller, M.W., (1993). Migration of cortical neurons is altered by gestational exposure to ethanol. *Alcoholism.* 17(2):304-314.

Norse, B.A., (1991). *Information processing: a conceptual approach to understanding the behavioral disorders of fetal alcohol syndrome.* Paper presented to International Conference on Education Children with Fetal Alcohol Syndrome. University of Alaska, Fairbanks.

Nanson, J.L., & Hiscock, M., (1990). Attention deficits in children exposed to alcohol prenatally. *Alcoholism.* 14(4):656-661.
Palmer, H.R., Ouellette, E.M., Warner, L., & Lichtman, S.R., (1974). Congenital malformations in offspring of a chronic alcoholic mother. *Pediatrics.* 53:490-494.

Pierog, S., Chandavasu, O., & Wexler, I., (1977). Withdrawal symptoms in infants with the fetal alcohol syndrome. *Journal of Pediatrics.* 90:630-633.

Randall, C., Anton, R.F., Becker, H.C., Hale, R.L., & Ekblad, U., (1992). Asprin dose-dependently reduces alcohol-induced birth defects and prostaglandin E levels in mice. *Teratology.* 44(5):521-529.

Redei, E., Clark, W.R., & McGivern, R.F., (1989). Alcohol exposure in utero results in diminished T-cell function and alterations in brain corticotropin-releasing factor and ACTH content. *Alcoholism.* 13(3):439-443.

Remkes, T., (1993). Saying no – completely. *Canadian Nurse.* 89(6):25-28.

Rool, A.W., Reiter, E.O., Andriola, M., & Duckett, G., (1975). Hypothalamic pituitary function in the fetal alcohol syndrome.

Rosengren, J., (1990). Alcohol. A bigger drug problem? *Minnesota Medicine.* 73(4):33-34.

Rosett, H.L., (1976). Effects of maternal drinking on child development: an introductory review. *Annals of the New York Academy of Sciences.* 273:115-117.

Russell, M., & Skinner, J.B., (1988). Early measures of maternal alcohol misuse as predictors of adverse pregnancy outcomes. *Alcoholism.* 12(6):824-830.

Sandor, G.S., Smith, D.F., & MacLeod, P.M., (1981). Cardiac malformations in the fetal alcohol syndrome. *Journal of Pediatrics.* 98:771-773.

Schorling, J.B., (1993). The prevention of prenatal alcohol use: a critical analysis of intervention studies. *Journal of Studies on Alcohol.* 543(3):261-267.

Smith, D.W., (1982). *Fetal alcohol effects (fetal alcohol syndrome).* Recognizable Patterns of Human Malformations. Sanders. 411-113.

Smith D.W., Jones, K.L., Hanson. J.W., & James, W., (1976). Perspectives on the fetal alcohol syndrome. *Annals of the New York Academy of Sciences.* 273:138-139.

Smith, I.E., & Coles, C.D., (1991). Multilevel intervention for prevention of fetal alcohol syndrome and effects of prenatal alcohol exposure. *Recent Developments in Alcoholism.* 9:165-180.

Smith, K.J. & Eckadt, M.J., (1991). The effects of prenatal alcohol on the central nervous system. *Recent Developments in Alcoholism.* 9:151-164.

Spohr, H.L., (1993). Prenatal alcohol exposure and long-term developmental consequences. *Lancet.* 341:907-910.

Steinmetz, G., (1992). The preventable tragedy: fetal alcohol syndrome. *National Geographic.* February.

Stephens, C.J., (1981). The fetal alcohol syndrome: cause for concern. *The American Journal of Maternal Child Nursing.* 6(4):151-156.

Streissguth, A.P., (1989). I.Q. at age four in relation to maternal alcohol use and smoking during pregnancy. *Developmental Psychology.* 25(10):3-11.

Streissguth, A.P., (1990). Prenatal alcohol-induced brain damage and long-term postnatal consequences: introduction to the symposium. *Alcoholism.* 14(5):648-649.

Streissguth, A.P., (1976) Psychologic Handicaps in children with the fetal alcohol syndrome. *Annals of the New York Academy of Sciences.* 273:140-145.

Streissguth, A.P., Aase, J.M., Clarren, S.K., Randels, S.P., LaDue R.A., & Smith, D.F. (1991). Fetal alcohol syndrome in adolescents and adults. *Journal of the American Medical Association.* 265(15):1961-1967.

Streissguth, A.P., Barr, H.M., Sampson, P.D., Bookstein, F.L., & Darby, B.L., (1990). Moderate prenatal alcohol exposure: effects on child I.Q. and learning problems at age 71/2. *Alcoholism.* 14(5):662-229.

Streissguth, A.P., Bookstein, F.L., Sampson, P.D., & Barr, H.M., (1989). Neurobehavioral effects of prenatal alcohol, 111:PLS analysis of neuropsychological tests. *Neurotoxicological Teratology.* 111:477-491.

Streissguth, A.P., Clarren, S.K., & Jones, K.L., (1985). Natural history of the fetal alcohol syndrome" a ten-year follow-up of eleven patients. *Lancet.* 2:85-92.

Streissguth, A.P., Herman, C.S., & Smith, D.W., ((1978). Intelligence, behavior, and dysmorphologenesis in the fetal alcohol syndrome: a report on 20 patients. *Journal of Pediatrics.* 92(3):363-367.

Streissguth, A.P., Herman, C.S., & Smith, D.W., (1978). Stability of intelligence in the fetal alcohol syndrome: a   preliminary report. *Alcohol Clin Exp Res.* 2:165-170.

Streissguth, A.P., LaDue, R.A., & Randels, S.P., (1988). *A manual on adolescents and adults with special reference to American Indians.* US Department of Health and Human Services.

Streissguth, A.P., Randels, S.P., & Smith, D.W., (1991). A test-retest study of intelligence in patients with fetal alcohol syndrome:

implications for care. *Journal of the American Academy of Child and Adolescent Psychiatry.* 30(4):145-158.

Streissguth, A.P., Sampson, P.D., & Barr, H.M., (1989). Neurobehavioral dose-response effects of prenatal alcohol exposure in humans from infancy to adulthood. *Annals of the New York Academy of Sciences.* 562:145-158.

Str:omland, K., (1990). Contribution of ocular examination to the diagnosis of foetal alcohol syndrome in mentally retarded children. *Journal of Mental Deficiency Research.* 34(5):429-435.

Ulleland, C.N., (1972). The offspring of alcoholic mothers. *Annals of the New York Academy of Sciences.* 197:167-169.

U.S. Deparment of Health and Human Services (1990). *Fetal alcohol syndrome and other effects of alcohol on pregnancy outcome.* Seventh Special Report to the U.S. Congress on Alcohol and Health from the secretary of Health and Human Services.

Warren, K.R., (1985). Alcohol-related birth defects: current trends in research. *Alcohol Health and Research World.* 4-5.

Warren, K.R., & Bast, R.J., (1988). Alcohol-related birth defects: an update. *Public Health Reports-Hyattsville.* 103(6):638-642.

Waterson, E.J. & Murray-Lyon, I.M. (1990). Preventing alcohol related birth damage: a review. *Social Science and Medicine.* 30(3):349-364.

Weinberg J., & Jerrells, T.R., (1991). Suppression of immune responsiveness: sex differences in prenatal ethanol effects. *Alcoholism.* 15(3):525-531.

Weiner, L., & Morse, B.A., (1991). *Facilitating development for children with fetal alcohol syndrome.* Child and Adolescent Behavior Letter, The Brown University.

Zidenberg-Cherr, S., Benak, P.A., Hurley, L.S., & Keen, C.L., (1988). Altered mineral metabolism: a mechanism underlying the fetal alcohol syndrome in rats. *Drug-Nutrition Interactions.* 5(4):257-274.